THE ENNEAGRAM:
A Journey of Self Discovery

by

Maria Beesing, O.P.
Robert J. Nogosek, C.S.C.
Patrick H. O'Leary, S.J.

Dimension Books, Inc.
Denville, New Jersey 07834

ACKNOWLEDGMENTS

The authors wish to express gratitude to all who have contributed to this work: to the readers of the manuscript in its various phases, especially Suzanne Brown, Sr. Anton Marie Voissem, SSND, Janet Schlichting, OP, and Joseph Zubricky, SJ; to Dolores Kratzer and Barbara Leggott for re-typing the manuscript; to Suzanne Brown for the cover design; to Suzanne Sliva for the artwork on the figures; to our friends and the many workshop participants who urged and supported us.

TABLE OF CONTENTS

PART TWO: Understanding One's Compulsion

PART THREE: Overcoming One's Compulsion

ILLUSTRATIONS OF THE ENNEAGRAM

INTRODUCTION

The Enneagram has a long but shrouded history. It is reputed to have originated in Afghanistan almost 2000 years ago, perhaps in the early years of Christian influence in Persia, and then to have infiltrated into Moslem circles after that religion invaded central Asia and the subcontinent of India. Until the present century it remained strictly an *oral tradition* known only to Sufi masters who would reveal to an individual disciple only the part of the Enneagram pertaining to that person's personality type. Oscar Ichazo is credited with bringing the Sufi Enneagram to public attention first in Chile and then in the United States. Ichazo grew up in Bolivia and Peru and was taught the Sufi tradition of the Enneagram in La Paz, Bolivia, by a man whose name he pledged not to reveal.[1] Some years later Ichazo attracted the attention of some members of the Esalen Institute of Big Sur, California, by his lectures at the Institute for Applied Psychology in Santiago, Chile. Among those persons from the Esalen Institute was Claudio Naranjo who later passed on the tradition of the Enneagram to Bob Ochs, S.J.

It was in a course on Religious Experience given by Bob Ochs at Loyola University in Chicago in 1971 that Pat O'Leary, S.J. was first introduced to the Enneagram system. Later, in the second semester of that school term, O'Leary participated in a seminar reflecting on the Enneagram with some other Jesuit priests under the leadership of Ochs. They sought to test its validity in the light of their own experience and

1

background in Ignatian spirituality. Out of this reflection O'Leary began teaching the Enneagram in workshops on spiritual direction. Maria Beesing, O.P., learned the Enneagram in 1974 and later joined O'Leary in developing his theories about the Enneagram. Based on their experiences as teachers, administrators, counselors and spiritual directors, Beesing and O'Leary have developed a series of workshops to teach and apply the Enneagram at Jesuit Retreat House in Cleveland, Ohio, and elsewhere.

The contribution of Fr. Robert Nogosek, C.S.C., to the writing of this book follows from his participation in three of these workshops. He sorted out the material of the workshops to compose a journey into the self in three stages: (1) discovering one's compulsion, (2) understanding its causes, and (3) overcoming the compulsion. He added to the workshop material reflections on the causes of the compulsions, derived in part from insights of Tad Dunne, S.J., and further implications of the Enneagram on the spiritual life, especially as derived from gospel values.

This book is intended to help persons see themselves in the mirror of their minds, especially to see the images of personality distorted by basic attitudes about self. To identify and admit this prevailing "compulsion" is to be open to see life more fully, provided that one is willing to address this "hidden sin" in one's behavior and to look directly to God for healing. Though the Enneagram is not meant to be a panacea for becoming holy, its careful study, preferably connected with making some Enneagram workshops, results in a new self-understanding and practical guidelines for achieving healing. This leads one to a greater personal freedom under the lead of the Spirit. The real story of the Enneagram is the journey each person makes by entering the amazing insight and wisdom underlying the simple diagram of THE EN-NEAGRAM.

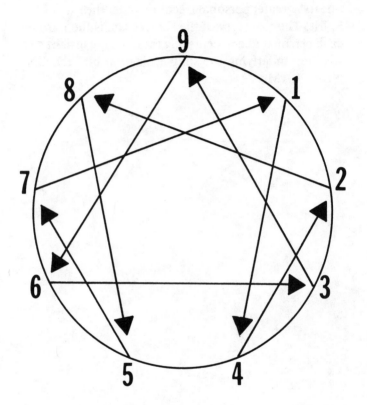

PART ONE:
Discovering One's Compulsion

1. FINDING ONESELF IN THE ENNEAGRAM

The Sufi Enneagram represents a *journey into self.* Although the Enneagram personality types may be discovered in friends, other acquaintances and even in past historical figures, the main purpose of the Enneagram is *to discover one's own type.* The result can be very rewarding. It can bring a whole new understanding of one's personality, which will be valid for the rest of one's life. Finding one's Enneagram type is meant to be a *self-enlightenment* which leads to authentic personal freedom on a level never before experienced.

The term "enneagram" is derived from the Greek word "enneas," meaning nine. According to the Enneagram system there are nine, and only nine, types of human personality. Each personality type is identified in a negative way though it also has positive characteristics. The identifying negativity stems from a specific *compulsion* ingrained in one's self-concept and having great influence on one's behavior.

The compulsion typical of a given personality is experienced as a *basic driving force.* It is not simply an obsession, such as a fixed idea or preoccupation of the consciousness. It has the characteristic of *prevailing* in the way energy is channeled in personal behavior, and even of being irresistible, especially when it remains hidden and unrecognized. The compulsion is a kind of "hidden sin," where sin is understood as a kind of paralysis or hindrance in becoming one's true authentic self.[3] It causes people not to understand themselves in their real motives and in the underlying drives of their personalities.

Discovering this compulsion characterizing one's personality involves the unveiling of the hidden but basic *defensive strategy* a person has developed for security and meaningful existence. This defensive strategy has been so carefully hidden that probably it is not consciously perceived or reflected upon by the person. As a result it is not known as constituting a *problem* needing attention as one makes efforts to achieve personal growth and fulfillment. To discover this "problem" through the Enneagram will result in a new freedom because now the person can freely decide *whether or not to follow the compulsion.* As long as the compulsion remains unnoticed such a choice is much less possible. When the driving force of the compulsion simply has not been faced head-on, it tends to go its merry way, having a great deal of influence on decisions made about what to do or not to do, how to think about oneself in relation to others, etc.

The journey into self offered by the Enneagram is *not easy.* To many it will turn out to be extremely threatening. It is unpleasant to think of one's basic personality as a "sin type." The compulsion serves to protect oneself and offers personal security. To seek to unveil it will be experienced as a kind of "death" to oneself in the form of willingness to allow investigation and criticism of one's consistent way of coping with life, which was probably quite fully developed already by the age of six years.[4] Even when identified through the Enneagram and dealt with through the various ways of achieving liberation and healing as presented in this book the negative personality type will remain. One will always have this sin type, even though it may eventually become more "redeemed" than compulsive.

In beginning this Enneagramic journey into the self what is being asked is the willingness to acknowledge oneself as a *sinner*. Compulsions are selfish as is typical of sin. They amount to a distortion in being as one ought to be. All the nine types are sin types; none is any less sinful than any other.

In their reluctance to face this negativity of the Enneagram people often seek to identify their personality with the cluster of gifts characteristic of a given type. In doing this they usually find themselves represented in a number of the types and end up saying they have some of this type, some of that type, etc. This is a way of skirting around the threat of recognizing any real compulsion or sin at all in themselves. As long as this continues to occur the Enneagram will be of little or no benefit. If the Enneagram is to be useful, one must discover the *negativity* of one's personality. Only then can one begin the process of being freed from the compulsion.

Some would argue that this desire to see one's personality as characterized by positive gifts should be made use of when introducing people to the Enneagram system. Since each type is indeed identifiable by a set of good qualities, why not begin by having people try to discover their personality type by its gifts? Such a tack, however, only delays the necessary pain of the real journey into self. The right way to become familiar with the Enneagram is to muster the sincerity and courage needed for any serious facing of the truth about oneself, the kind of truth that can set one free.[5]

Through the discovery of one's Enneagram type there can be awakened a whole new sense of *self-criticism*. It will give one always something to repent, something to confess as sin, something to make resolutions about for the future. This self-criticism will in itself already be a basic step to that new freedom promised by the Enneagram, a freedom from being secretly led by the *dark side* of one's inner self.

The discovery of one's type will also point out a *lack of faith* on a deep level. Underlying the compulsion of each type is a way of defending the self which is selfish and disruptive of bondedness with others. As a strategy for self-protection it is a chosen way of "self-salvation." The personality has simply chosen a way to achieve security and fulfillment by its own efforts. This is, of course, a *mistake.* Through the discovery of one's Enneagram type there can be awakened a whole new sense of *needing salvation,* instead of simply having to rely on one's own stratagems and resources for personal fulfillment.

As has been said, each personality type is characterized by a strategy to defend and protect the self. This means that the compulsion is fundamentally the *avoidance* of something. Its *power* in one's life is felt precisely in this avoidance. This is generally not recognized for the problem it is; indeed, it is often labeled as something one can be *proud of.* Although people are not generally proud of what they call their sins, they do tend to be proud of the compulsion characterizing their personality type. They think it makes them superior to those who do not have this compulsion.

All this suggests that to undertake this journey into self through the Enneagram is a *very big step* which can have tremendous consequences on how one views oneself, God and others. It opens whole new horizons of awareness concerning what is going on in one's personality, thereby enabling it to be tapped into and dealt with.

The Avoidance of Each Personality Type

The investigation of the Enneagram begins with the study of each type according to its specific avoidance. The types are numbered 1 through 9 on a circle within which are interlocking figures. Although names could be given for each type and eventually will be given in the course of this book, it remains best to identify them simply by their *numbers,* to speak of "ONES," "TWOS," etc. In this way the door is left open to whatever content is to be discovered in each type through experience. FIGURE 1 illustrates the avoidances of each personality type on the Enneagram.

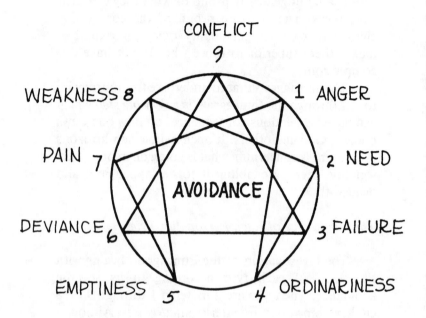

FIGURE 1

#1. ONES avoid *anger.* Although they do perceive much to be distressed or upset about, it is very important to them not to become angry and not to express anger to others. They are very dedicated to being *perfect* and to doing things in a perfect way. For this they are ready to work very hard preparing their tasks, cleaning the house, etc. They are bothered when things are not done right, whether by themselves or by others.

#2. TWOS avoid recognizing they have *needs.* They readily see needs in others; indeed, they are preoccupied in noticing what needs others have. They pride themselves in being *helpful*, especially to anyone special to them. As regards themselves they do not admit they need others for any help, nor that they have needs which they should attend to themselves. It is important to them not to admit being in need.

#3. THREES avoid *failure.* Something drives them to be always working for *success* in their lives. Their personality actually identifies with the successes they attain. Consequently, they will seek to avoid failure of any sort, even at great cost to themselves and others.

#4. FOURS avoid *ordinariness.* It is very important to them always to be *special.* They experience themselves as persons of refinement and sensitivity and in no way simply as ordinary persons. They are inclined to think others do not understand them because of the *uniqueness* of the feelings they have experienced, especially concerning the sorrow and even tragedy of their lives.

#5. FIVES avoid *emptiness.* They are preoccupied with growing in their *store of knowledge,*

which they seek to acquire wholly through their own efforts. They feel a deep need to know more than they ever say to others, as though sharing everything would leave them with nothing. It is very important not to get caught in social involvements which are boring to them, i.e., not helpful for learning something.

#6. SIXES avoid *deviance.* They see life as governed by laws, rules and norms. Out of *responsibility* to the demands life makes on them they strive to avoid any neglect of their duties. They are preoccupied that all regulations be observed, especially those given by a person in authority or set down in writing. They see this in terms of *loyalty* to the group or groups to which they belong.

#7. SEVENS avoid *pain.* They are optimistic and *fun-loving* persons, and to them life should not be experienced as painful in any way. They avoid noticing pain or distress in the lives of others around them. Often they fail to carry out what they have planned to do because of the difficulties and discomforts involved in its execution.

#8. EIGHTS avoid *weakness.* They glory in being *strong* persons. They perceive life as a struggle for what is right. The fact that the world is not the way it should be means that to keep their personal dignity they must be ready to meet head-on whatever is wrong and unmask its injustice and pretenses. They like to "have it out" with others. They are watchful not to be taken advantage of, and take extreme care not to let others see them as weak in any way.

#9. NINES avoid *conflict.* They feel uncomfortable with any tension or lack of harmony between people. To them nothing is as important as *peace* and

restraint. They have a lot of concern not only to maintain their own inner tranquility, which is fairly easy to do, but also to keep peace among those around them. They feel a need for others to draw them into activity, otherwise they lack incentive to do things.

Description of Each Personality Type

It is now time to look at a fuller description of each type, first in its negative aspects and then in its positive gifts. At the end of each description is a list of statements characteristic of each type, a form of a self-examination. These statements are adapted from Jerry Wagner's "Enneagram Personality Inventory."[6] In reading the descriptions it is well to go first to one's own type, which hopefully has been discovered through perusal of the *avoidances.* Should the reader have been able to narrow down the possible types to only two or three, the statements of self-examination will be particularly helpful in selecting which one of these is most characteristic of one's personality. Only after the study of one's own Enneagram type should the descriptions of all the other types be read. This prior acknowledgement of one's own "sin type" will aid the understanding and acceptance of the other compulsions as other "sin types." In this way the discoveries made through the Enneagram can serve to build union with others through the common recognition that all persons are sinners, rather than have the recognition of their compulsions intensify dislike or even hostility towards them. Compulsions are always best understood and experienced from within the self. One can *guess* at the motives and drives of others but that is not to know them in their actual consciousness.

#1

ONES avoid anger because they are perfectionists. They do not allow themselves the "imperfection" of becoming angry. They do have anger, of course, but it is suppressed, even to the point of not being consciously known or felt. Often there will be a tone of irritation in their voices and an edginess in their behavior. To intimate friends they will often express *resentment* about the faults in others and the hurts they have received from them.

Because of the expectation ONES have that life should be perfect, they tend to be preoccupied with an attitude that things are never as they should be. They feel resentment about this but ordinarily react to it by trying doubly hard themselves to get things right. They spend much time reviewing and preparing what needs to be done, tidying up the house, etc. They are the classic perfect housekeepers, meticulous accountants and teachers who insist that lessons be done over if they are not done right the first time. They are always ready to spend extra time on a task since it is so important to them that it be done well. Since the perfection they insist on is viewed by them as attainable, they will work hard at making it happen.

The great importance they give to perfection often leads them into frustration and dissatisfaction with what they see in themselves and in their surroundings. They greatly overdo the value of perfection, especially in view of the limitations of time and of human nature, but they are not ready to accept this truth. To them it is not right to have things imperfect. They see themselves as always *trying* to do what is right and they expect others to do so as well. It bothers them that another does not seem to try nearly as hard as they do to correct things and make them right.

A good question is why do they always need things to be perfect? The answer is that according to their viewpoint they are acceptable as persons only when they are perfect. They have simply grown up with the idea that *unless they are perfect they are not acceptable.* Typically as children they were the "good boy" or the "good girl." They have an *inner critic* which continually checks possible faults, much like the control room monitors the TV announcer through an earphone. Because of this inner critic they often answer criticism of themselves which seems to come from nowhere. They even interrupt themselves in the middle of a sentence to answer an objection. They have a penchant to review the past in detail, especially the day just lived, even to the point of analyzing what happened at each moment. They like the details of the past and in a journal are likely to note the exact time, even to the minute, when they were wakened from sleep or when someone arrived to meet them. This is all in line with checking out whether what they did was right or wrong. They will also tend to do this sort of thing at meetings with others. They will be sticklers for looking over the past in detail lest something be missed that needs to be seen. Meanwhile the others will be chewing their fingernails waiting to get on with the agenda and to make some decisions for the future.

In analyzing the past ONES go back over the old arguments again and again, often bringing up the same doubts and objections, even though others have long considered the matter to have been settled. It is difficult for ONES to put to rest any issue of right or wrong. This is because the inner critic is ever ready to bring up the old objections and never seems completely satisfied about the goodness or rightness of anything. Objections to past behavior are apt to come up at any time, even completely out of context with what is going on at present. This dissatisfaction in ONES causes them to be restless and "on edge." They seem "high-strung." Suppressed frustration causes an irritability in the voice. What was at fault in the past is kept bottled up inside and new faults in themselves or others are added to the collection of faults they keep thinking about.

ONES, of course, are not aware that anger is being suppressed, even though they are bothered by whatever is not perfect. The faults and shortcomings of others are seen as quite unacceptable but typically ONES do not tell another what his or her faults are. That person is expected to be aware of the faults and to correct them. Such a stance toward others tends to make ONES poorly adapted to their environment. There is an unspoken *intolerance* for the way things are. They constantly are thinking about the improvement needed both by themselves and others. People experience ONES as generally *dissatisfied* about something.

There is also in ONES a stubbornness in having things done their way. They tend to be impatient with traditional, "time-tested" procedures. They see some very simple and direct way of doing a thing and will try to manipulate others to have it done this way. The details on *how a thing is done* are very important to them. It can, of course, blind them to greater values.

They tend "not to see the forest for the trees," getting so bogged down in the details of a task that they fail to ask whether any of it should be done in the first place!

This *meticulousness* about details causes them to be very slow in making decisions. They insist that a decision not be made until *all the details* have been studied. In seeking their cooperation it is wise not to spring on them the necessity of making an instant decision, for then their response will probably be negative. It does not seem to them there is enough time to think about whether this is the right thing or the wrong thing to do. As group leaders they will not be able to begin a business meeting until every member has arrived. From their viewpoint, the group cannot function at all until it is perfect, i.e., with all the members present.

ONES apologize often to others. They say, "I'm no expert at this. I didn't get this done the way it should have been done. There was just not enough time to do this right." Here they are simply expressing dissatisfaction with themselves. It does not seem to them that there is ever enough time to get things done just right. They can't tolerate sloppiness; they will say, "There is a place for everything and everything should be in its place." As long as they keep trying to do things according to their own standards of perfection, they are basically healthy psychologically. A real problem arises, however, when they feel overwhelmed by a mountain of work. Once they perceive that there is neither time nor energy to do any of their tasks really well, they are likely to become very discouraged and may even fall into moodiness and depression. As a result they will end up doing practically nothing at all, except feel sullen and trampled upon by others.

Along with all this compulsiveness they do have many endearing qualities. They are to be admired for always trying to be perfect. As children they were probably very faithful in doing school work, even at the sacrifice of having fun. They will make almost any sacrifice to do things right. They are willing to put in many extra hours for the work of preparation and give great attention to neatness and orderliness.

As companions ONES can be much fun for they are often very amusing and entertaining. They are animated in speaking and have a charming simplicity in the way they make a point or get a point. They *point* often as they talk. Their insistence on taking all details seriously can make quite ordinary events, such as the exact time something happened, things significant to talk about and remember. They are very much in touch with daily life. The fact that they keep thinking about all that needs to be made better can challenge others in an engaging way to make more efforts at improvement. Their concern for order and neatness certainly will make any place more fitting and attractive for human habitation.

They are to be especially appreciated for their *honesty* and *directness*. They insist on fairness to all. Although often people cater to those who have power or wealth, ONES see right through all pretences of superiority and are ready to treat each person equally. They help their friends become authentic persons, for that is what ONES expect of everyone.

Those who are ONES will probably agree with most of the following statements:[7]

1. I put much effort into correcting my faults.
2. I'm often bothered because things aren't the way they should be.
3. I hate to waste time.
4. I often blame myself for not doing better.
5. Often the least flaw can ruin the whole thing for me.
6. I have trouble relaxing and being playful.
7. Voices critical of me and others frequently chatter in my head.
8. I seem to worry more than other people.
9. I feel almost compelled to be honest.
10. I sometimes sense a Puritanical streak in myself.
11. Being right is important for me.
12. I frequently have a sense of urgency that time is running out and there is still so much left to do.
13. I feel a need to be accountable for most of my time.
14. I could easily be, or am, a scrupulous person.
15. I can identify rather easily with crusaders against evil.
16. If something isn't fair, it *really* bothers me.
17. I feel almost compelled to keep trying to better myself and what I am doing.
18. I feel I have to be perfect before others will love me or approve of me.
19. I frequently feel frustrated because neither I nor others are the way we should be.
20. I seem to see things in terms of right or wrong, good or bad.

#2

TWOS avoid acknowledging their own needs; instead, they are always busy meeting the needs of others. Behind this spirit of being a *helper* they do have a deep need to get something in return from the person being helped. What they are looking for in return, without probably consciously realizing it, is love and appreciation, especially as expressed in a *dependency* of others on them. They are really very needy persons. The reason for all their concern to help another is to get attention from that person. This is their tactic of *winning love.* Their blindness to this being a tactic comes from the way they avoid admitting their real motives of personal need as they go about serving another.

TWOS "need to be needed." Their attention will be on ways to respond to others' needs, especially to someone important to them. On one occasion while playing doubles on a tennis court without adequate fencing, the TWO's main concern was to run after balls that went out of bounds! Such concern to serve the needs of others is the primary way the TWO has of relating. Often TWOS will take pains to find out what a friend's favorite things are, so as to know what food to prepare or what clothes to wear to please the friend when he or she comes to visit. The friend is expected to notice what was done to please. Not to notice results in the TWO becoming considerably upset with deep feelings of hurt. The friend can be mystified by this and may remark to the TWO about "making a mountain out of a molehill." TWOS do not ordinarily confront others openly with anger but express their annoyance at being "scorned" by saying, perhaps tearfully, that they are not appreciated for all they have done. They may even take revenge by making belittling remarks about their friend to others.

For TWOS time is valued mainly in terms of being used for personal relationships. At a meeting they focus on some way to attend to other persons or to get their attention, perhaps by serving coffee. They measure the worthwhileness of a meeting by how well they relate to some of the persons present, rather than by how much of the agenda is accomplished.

Since they think of themselves as being helpers, their chosen career is often that of a helping profession. In that work there is the danger that they may become much too intent on making personal relationships with those being helped. They may attempt to do this by various kinds of manipulation to make the other dependent on the services they can render, so that the personal intimacy continues. In all this they feel quite proud of being self-sacrificing for another. As counsellors they want the client to be pleased with the sessions and tend to center only on those needs which they can care for from their own resources of friendliness and advice.

Their compulsion of needing to be needed puts them at a great disadvantage when others do not need help or simply resent being helped. No matter how needy some persons are, they simply resist being put into the dependency situation the TWO seeks to create. What happens if there is indeed no one for the TWO to help? According to the outlook of the TWO, *when there is nothing to do for others, there is nothing to do at all.*

It is easy to see and admire the positive qualities characteristic of TWOS. They are kind, sensitive and concerned about what is good for others. They are ready to make great sacrifices to help. They set a high value on personal relationships. They are warm, tactile persons; they want to touch others, to take them by the hand and make them comfortable and happy. They are always ready to welcome another into their home. Far from living in their own world, they take intimate notice of other persons wherever they meet them and want them to feel important and very much loved.

They talk much about the needs of others. They are ready to go anywhere to help others in the family or even those outside the family. They have much *sympathy* and move out to people with feeling and with open and outstretched arms. No wonder they are often thought of by others as "living saints!"

TWOS are naturally non-violent. They may even have a happy *innocence* about the real evils of the world. Instead of condemning others for their mistakes, moral or otherwise, they try to help them in the misfortunes resulting from the mistakes. For the TWO what is important is to help others, not to judge or condemn them.

Twos will probably agree to most of the following statements:[8]

1. Many people depend on my help and generosity.
2. I take more pride in my service of others than in anything else.
3. I need to feel important in other people's lives. I like people to need me.
4. Many people feel close to me.
5. I regularly compliment other people.
6. I like to rescue people when I see they're in trouble or are in embarrassing situations.
7. I'm almost compelled to help other people, whether I feel like it or not.
8. People often come to me for comfort and advice.
9. Many times I feel overburdened by others' dependence on me.
10. I don't feel that I have that many needs.
11. I sometimes feel that others really don't appreciate me for what I've done for them.
12. I like to feel "close" to people.
13. Sometimes I feel victimized by others, as though I'm just being used by them.
14. To love and be loved are the most important things in life.
15. Emotional issues are important to me.

16. I feel I deserve to be first in someone's life because of all I've done for them.
17. I think of myself as a nurturing kind of person.
18. When I have time off, I frequently spend it helping others.
19. I communicate with my friends more often than they communicate with me.
20. I like taking care of others.

#3

The compulsion of the THREE is to avoid failure. THREES grew up thinking their own personal worth consisted simply in the success of their achievements. As a consequence, they tend to put their whole identity as persons into the role they have. They may change roles in life but they value their whole life in terms of success in the role they presently have. From the way they look at themselves, failure is intolerable. They put all their energy into succeeding in the task or role they have undertaken though ordinarily they undertake only what has a very good chance of succeeding and do not take on what could be risky.

To them success includes *efficiency*. They are concerned about doing things in the best way possible. They see success as depending on good organization and planning. They insist on writing out goals and objectives and are sticklers for evaluation of performance. Since the success of their enterprise is all important, they not only sacrifice their own lives for it, but also expect others to be willing to make similar personal sacrifices. They demand of their employees a job well done and have a hard time understanding the inefficiency and apparent waste of time in the performance of some people. They tend to be quite intolerant of any incompetence in others.

Crucial to success as they see it is the image projected before the public eye. As salespersons they believe completely in the product they are selling. They may not even recognize that the sincerity they are projecting may not be the truth they know deep down in their hearts. To their thinking they are sincere, for their hearts are engrossed in projecting an image that will sell the product. Almost unconsciously in public they *put on* feelings they see as appropriate for success. As a consequence they sacrifice their own innate feelings for the sake of creating an image before others. They tend not to have a private and personal life but get caught up in their role and in what they are trying to achieve. They do have strong personal feelings but these are put aside to be considered at some other time. After all, they do not want to let their personal feelings get in the way of the success they are working for! As a result, they typically wear a mask, the Jungian *persona*, which portrays their role but does not let others know them personally. They wear this mask without noticing it since they have so much identified themselves with their role.

THREES like to choose a profession where they can run their own show. They become salespersons, business executives or even physicians. Whatever their role, it constitutes their real life. They so much identify with their enterprise that they tend to overlook the contributions of others to its success. Others are sometimes manipulated as instruments for getting work done or as stepping stones to success. They can be quite cold when they are concerned with what they see as their success, and they have a need to pile one success upon the other as though no one success could ever be enough.

They generally display a great drive to activity. Should they not have a goal clearly in mind or know what to do next, they still keep moving even though it is only by shuffling papers around or pacing the floor. Because their drive to activity is so strong, it would be unhealthy for them to decide to do nothing, no matter what the reasons.

Many of the values so important to THREES are greatly admired and needed by others. The great effort they make to get everything organized is a real gift to others. Their insistence on clearly defined goals, job descriptions and standards for evaluating success or failure draws people to work together and share a common spirit. They don't fuss much about details, but continually place before others in the organization the purpose of the work and a vision for the future. Their great determination to succeed generates energy to expand the work and involve even more people to collaborate in the enterprise.

THREES are good team persons. The lively image they radiate stirs others into activity and creates a sense of satisfaction in working for something really worthwhile. Their *enthusiasm* is quite contagious. They spur others to put more care into outward appearances and into smooth cooperative action. Their strong motivation keeps people on their toes and enkindles greater efforts for the common endeavor.

They are ordinarily great *talkers*. They seem never to run out of words. They make their presence both animating and entertaining for others. They can take a truth and make it sound really great. Since they are attention-getters, they will have a pleasing appearance in every way, including the way they dress.

To work for a THREE can bring out the best in a person. THREES are not clock-watchers, expecting everyone to punch in and out at exactly the right time. They will not fuss about lack of punctuality or the need of a person to go home early, provided that the job gets done. Their great dedication to success gives considerable assurance to anyone joining their organization that this will be a winning team.

They also make good counselors or spiritual directors. They are very objective and can help others get their lives organized according to some worthwhile goals. They challenge others to sort out what they are living for and to take appropriate steps to live according to their hopes and convictions.

THREES will probably agree to most of the following statements:[9]

1. I like to keep myself on the go.
2. I like to work on a team and I make a good team member.
3. I identify with precision and professionalism.
4. Being able to get things organized and accomplished just seems to come natural to me.
5. "Success" is a word that means a lot to me.
6. I like to have clear goals set and to know where I stand on the way toward those goals.
7. I like progress charts, grades and other indications of how I am going.
8. I'm envied by other people for how much I get done.
9. Projecting a successful image is very important to me.
10. Making decisions is not a problem for me.
11. To be successful you sometimes have to compromise your own standards.
12. When I recall my past, I tend to remember what I did well and right rather than what I did poorly or wrong.
13. I hate to be told something I'm doing isn't working.
14. Generally, I prefer to be involved in the aspect of an operation that will get it moving rather than keep it going.
15. I would do well in the advertising aspect of a project.

16. I can get so identified with my work or role that I forget who *I* am.
17. I believe that appearances are important.
18. I feel I need many achievements before other people will notice me.
19. I tend to be an assertive go-getter kind of person.
20. First impressions count.

#4

The compulsion of FOURS is to avoid being ordinary. This means they feel they are very different from other people. This difference is especially due to a sense of the *tragic* in their lives. Often this was occasioned by growing up feeling abandoned by one or both parents. They feel that others do not understand the loneliness and other sufferings they have gone through. This sense of personal tragedy makes them feel *special* as persons.

It is difficult for them to feel natural and spontaneous. They may rehearse how they want to be before others, like an actor. They never feel they have attained the casualness they desire to have. Others experience them as having a "studied charm." Often they are painfully aware of playing a role, of acting before others, rather than just being themselves. They crave simplicity but never seem to attain it. They love the theatre; but while attending a performance, they identify with the acting rather than experience the play as a way to enter more deeply into life itself.

They have a smile that says they are special, that they understand some things better than others do. This gives them a certain air of superiority or aloofness even though they seem warm and friendly. They are not easy to get to know well. They dress in understatement, but with considerable taste and elegance. Even their body language says they are special, that others do not have as good taste or style, nor feel as deeply about things.

FOURS seem always to be looking forward to beginning their real lives. They envy others who seem more natural than they are, but they expect that once their life truly begins they will discover how to be natural. They feel they have not yet become deeply enough involved in feeling to be really alive. What makes them feel truly alive is intensity of emotion, whether of joy or sorrow. They crave deep feeling. To feel neutral would be to them to be only half-alive. They find it terribly difficult to say goodbye because they try to enter deeply into the tragic emotions of departure. Feelings of sadness, pain and other misfortunes captivate their attention. They are inclined to go back over the sad aspects of their past, deploring lost opportunities, an unhappy childhood or other experiences of hurt, loneliness or abandonment by others. This can make them moody and they can lose a sense of hope in life.

Their very specialness makes it difficult for them to enter into intimate relationships which, of course, depend on mutuality and equality. Since they have a penchant for feeling misunderstood, they will draw others to themselves and yet not let them into their real inner space. It may be thought that they enjoy depicting themselves as engulfed in tragedy; but as they explain what they have gone through, they are trying to say how special they feel themselves to be.

FOURS are attractive persons because of many remarkable qualities. They have very compassionate hearts. They know what pain is and what it feels like to be misunderstood or abandoned. Because of their great sensitivity they deeply feel hurts that others might not even notice or care about.

Another great quality they have is their innate sense of symbolic expression that goes beyond what any words can convey. Just being around them heightens a person's awareness of what is beautiful, tasteful, elegant and poetical. They often choose to be poets, musicians, actors or artists in some other way. They can be creative not only in how they express their feelings but also in the way they shape their immediate environment. Their ease in being original, for example, in the way they decorate their rooms, encourages others to try to put an original stamp on things rather than just to follow what others do.

FOURS are generally *charming* as personalities. They show good taste and elegant manners, far removed from everything crass or boorish. Though it may be difficult to know them really well, their very difference and originality make them a special gift to others just by their presence.

FOURS will probably agree with most of the following statements:[10]

1. Most people don't appreciate the real beauty of life.
2. I have an almost compulsive nostalgia for my past.
3. I try to look casual and natural.
4. I have always had an attraction for symbolism.
5. People don't feel as deeply as I do.
6. Other people often lack the capacity to understand how I feel.
7. I like to do things properly and with class.
8. My environmental surroundings are very important for me.

9. I like the theater very much and fantasize myself as being on the stage.
10. Manners and good taste are important to me.
11. I don't like to think of myself as being ordinary.
12. I can get preoccupied with suffering, loss and death.
13. I'm sometimes afraid that just my normal feeling response won't be enough.
14. I seem to absorb rather easily most of the feelings of a group, so much so that frequently I lose a sense of where my own feelings leave off and where others' begin.
15. I seem to be more bothered than most about the termination of relationships.
16. I resonate with the "tragic clown" figure, smiling through the gloom.
17. I have been accused of being aloof.
18. I find myself swinging back and forth between highs and lows. Either I'm very up or very down. I don't feel very alive when I'm in the middle.
19. People have accused me of being overly dramatic, but they really don't understand how I feel.
20. The arts and artistic expression are very important for me as a means of channeling my emotions.

#5

FIVES have a compulsion to avoid emptiness. Often they project outward their feeling of inner emptiness so that they consider others to be shallow in their thinking. In order to fill up their own emptiness FIVES withdraw from others physically or mentally in order to think and to reconstruct reality in some kind of pattern of meaning. They are *observers* of life much more than participants. Even when they attempt to move out of their aloneness, they seem to stand at the *periphery* of events rather than to become deeply involved in what is happening. They take pains to know what is going on without exactly being in it.

Their *silence* is often annoying to others. They seem to know much more than they ever say. Often they wait until the very end of a meeting before saying anything and then sum up everything that was said in a brilliant resume. When they do share what they have been thinking about, they present something like a treatise: they give an outline in distinct points and take pains to make each point patently clear. Since this kind of disclosure is often not quite appropriate for table conversation or the like, the boredom it causes others gives FIVES the feeling that others are too shallow to be interested in what they have to say. This makes FIVES prone to lapse back into silence. In any case, they will say only a part of what they know. To say everything would leave them with a feeling of being very empty.

As keen observers of reality they take in everything and store it inside. It is very important to them not to be stupid. They want to know all aspects of a subject or situation before they feel ready to say anything about it. Since a great deal of time is needed for all this study and reflection, they treasure the time they have for their projects and do not want it taken away from them by the intrusions of others. This makes them very guarded about their privacy. They need private space in order to know reality. What they mean by "reality" is a *correctness of judgment* concerning what is observable. Without that inner truth of judgment they will feel ignorant. To come to that correct judgment they insist on going through the process of study and research *all alone.*

This craving to fill an inner emptiness with knowledge often is the consequence of a childhood spent in loneliness and parental abandonment, especially through poor mother contact. As children they probably felt different from all the other members of the family, and even may have had lingering doubts about being the real offspring of their parents. For whatever reason they learned early to cope with their lonely feelings by withdrawing into their own world, which was filled with the information they had perceived and stored. They looked for opportunities to go apart from others to think things out for themselves. To them life came to consist more in reflection and understanding than in involvement and interaction with others. They withdraw in order to know, and this knowledge gives them a sense of fulfillment. Above all they want to avoid being foolish. Since it takes a great deal of time to become wise, they are always preparing themselves so that what they eventually express will be well thought out and true.

Their reserve and non-commitment can be irksome to others. Often they seem lost in their own thoughts. They have a poor sense of the present and this causes them to forget names and even fail to recognize persons with whom they have been recently. At social gatherings they are very uncomfortable in trying to make small talk. To escape the boredom they unobtrusively leave without saying why, or even saying goodbye. Just as silently they may drop into a gathering and simply be there as the others carry on. To them time is very precious, and if something is not beneficial to them they see no reason to continue to waste their time with it.

Their characteristic tendency to withdraw from others to be alone with their thoughts causes them often to feel they are outside of what is going on. They want to belong and be a part of social life with others but at the same time they are not ready to sacrifice their aloofness for this. They are hedgey about commitments to others for these may entail giving up precious time to be alone. They need to be *loners* in order not to feel drained and empty. This makes them inclined to avoid looking to others for help. Characteristically they work things out for themselves and then communicate with others about their conclusions. Only in that way do they feel life can be kept in proper perspective.

FIVES tend to be *stingy* with their time and with what they have learned. It does not occur to them that whatever is received as knowledge is to be shared with others. They value knowledge as a treasure in itself which fills their inner emptiness, irrespective of whether or not it is communicated to others. They build up their own resources of knowledge as something to be kept.

When their admirers tell them they must know much about something since they do so much reading, they probably say they really have not had time to learn all about it. This is not false humility; it really is the way they perceive the situation. To them there is never enough time to know anything well, i.e., from every point of view, which is the way they consider it needs to be known if anyone is going to be able to say much about it. When they are asked how they feel, they will probably respond in terms of what they *think*. Reality is perceived by them according to what is *significant* rather than according to what is felt. They are not devoid of deep feelings but they do not think that these are as important as what they know about something. Often they may simply want to keep their feelings unexpressed. In any case, it is difficult for them to be in touch with their feelings for they do not ordinarily live on an emotional level. When they speak, people notice their voice has little variation of feeling. This comes from the way FIVES *compartmentalize* their lives.

They do have many attractive qualities. They are very perceptive listeners. As parents they have the ability to draw out the hearts of their children and take great interest in the underlying significance of whatever their children experience. They like to delegate responsibility and to encourage others to make their own decisions and to do things for themselves. They are gentle as persons and are soft-spoken almost to a fault.

Another attractive quality of FIVES is that they find life *full of meaning.* They look for a pattern in events and deeper meanings underlying the ordinary. They make a great effort to communicate clearly with others when they do speak and to boil down complex matters into concise and understandable language. It is always important to them that everything be understood.

They are also non-critical persons. Their approach to reality is not from a stance of judgment, whether something be right or wrong, good or bad. To them everything is *interesting* to know. They see that it takes a long time to know anything and there are many aspects to any matter that need to be taken into account before anyone can make a valid judgment. Such a non-judgmental approach to life also gives them a special *wit* which tends to be a sense of the absurd.

They are able to find humor in almost anything in a wry sort of way which others will generally appreciate very much, especially since it pops up so unexpectedly.

FIVES will probably agree with most of the following statements:[11]

1. I tend to keep my feelings to myself.
2. I hold onto what I have and gather items I might need to use some day.
3. I don't know how to engage in small talk very well.
4. Intellectually I like to synthesize and put together different ideas.
5. I go blank when I'm embarrassed or when someone asks how I feel right now.
6. I need much private time and space.
7. I tend to let others take the initiative.
8. I often sit back and observe other people rather than get involved.
9. I tend to be something of a loner.
10. I seem to be more silent than most others. People often ask me what I'm thinking.
11. I have trouble reaching out or asking for what I need.
12. If an issue comes up, I like to first work it out by myself, then go discuss it with others.
13. Asserting myself is very difficult.
14. I try to solve my problems by thinking.
15. I like to put things in perspective, to step back and take everything in. If I leave anything out, I accuse myself of being so simplistic or naive.
16. I tend to be stingy with my time, money and self.
17. I really hate it when I don't get my money's worth.
18. When I'm upset with myself or others, I frequently think of myself or them in terms of "fools," "idiots," "stupid," etc.
19. I have a very soft tone of voice and people often have to ask me to speak up. This irritates me.
20. I tend to be more a taker than a giver.

#6

SIXES experience life as making great demands on them. These demands come from the expectations of others, especially from any group to which they belong. As a result they live in great apprehension and with many fears.

As children they probably experienced their father or a father-figure as very strict with them. School meant they were to conform to their teacher's demands and even suggestions. They grew up with the attitude that outside authority is to decide all issues. They are very concerned with *obeying* whatever is demanded by law.

They have a great need that there be no ambiguity in what is right or what is wrong. To achieve this they appeal to the rules or documents of an institution. Outside such authority or legitimation they lack self-confidence in making decisions. This clinging to authority is, of course, for the sake of *security*. The authority defines what is to be done and not done and how others are to be. Within the latitude of the law they move quite freely but they are likely to be very stubborn regarding any going beyond the norms. They say, "That is going too far. That is too far out."

Since they identify with group norms, they have a great need to belong to a specific group. They want to know who belongs to the group and who does not. In this way they tend to divide the world into "them" and "us." They even tend to be paranoid about possible threats to their group's well-being, as though threats might come from anywhere. They are very watchful that there be no deviance from the rules and norms of the group. Any such deviance by another is perceived by them as very wrong and they do not hesitate to point out who or what is deviant. They are very sure of themselves in demanding that all in their group conform to the rules of the group. Although they themselves may break such rules and norms, they do not readily admit this even to themselves.

They have a hard time knowing what to do with free time. They see time as to be used to fulfill some responsibility shown by an outside authority. They do want to use all their time in a responsible way, but if they are not shown clearly what is demanded of them they are uncertain what to do. Even in making a purchase at the store they may be very hesitant in deciding what to select and feel the need to ask someone else's opinion, even a stranger's. They often cover up uncertainty regarding what to do by much hyperactivity, which accomplishes little or nothing.

SIXES simply are not self-starters. Although they are ready for hard work, they need direction from the outside. *It is very important to them not to make the wrong decision.* This makes them very cautious. Often they simply avoid making a decision even though "not to decide is to decide." They may avoid risks to such an extent that they suffer from many lost opportunities in life.

A major problem for them is *insecurity.* They experience much fear and anxiety. There always seems to be something to be apprehensive about. Often what is feared is simply the unknown, the uncertain future. They feel much more secure with the "tried and tested" of the past than with experimenting with new ways of doing things. What others might consider a delightful challenge or adventure, SIXES view as threatening. They prefer to repeat what they have done very well in the past. They lack confidence in abilities they may actually have but have never used, at least not in this way. Simply stated they are *afraid of change.* This is due to a deep lack of self-confidence in their own ability to make good decisions or try new things. They experience life as full of dangers and demands. This means to them that they must be *very careful* in whatever they do regarding their responsibilities. Since they think there will be trouble if they do not conform to what is expected, caution is needed. Serious reading also poses a threat to them. Somehow they feel responsible for knowing everything they read. Every word in print is seen as important and as making some demand on them. Such a compulsion in feeling responsible for what is read is, of course, a great obstacle to learning. It often prevents them from doing much reading at all.

Often they sense that the best approach to danger is a *strong offense.* Feeling insecure, they are apt to consider any opposition to themselves or to their group as very dangerous or even malicious. To protect themselves they combat it vigorously, often by bringing out arguments in the form of threats "in the name of the law." Another way of taking the offensive is by using the word "never." They will say, "I will *never* allow that," or even "I will *never* change."

All this insecurity because of the perceived demands of life tends to make SIXES very serious persons and rather humorless. They may wish they did not take life so seriously but their compulsion to responsibility leads them that way. Apprehension and fear keep cropping up. Even though their past experience shows that often their fears were unwarranted and things actually turned out well, they continue to fear the future.

SIXES communicate genuine hospitality. They are very *loyal* persons and are wholeheartedly dedicated to whatever group they belong. With this loyalty comes a warmth of devotion and fellowship. They see the life of the group as very important and will make great sacrifices for it. They can function well in an executive or leadership position because they have a great sense of responsibility and devotion to the group. To do well in such a position they need *guidelines* that are appropriate, clear and unambiguous. Once they know what is expected of them they are very hard workers. Others are often amazed at the speed, accuracy and sheer output of their work. They take pains in being punctual as employees, and ordinarily do not mind working overtime as long as those in authority know they are doing so.

SIXES probably will agree with most of the following statements:[12]

1. I am basically a middle-of-the-road person.
2. Loyalty to a group is very important for me.
3. I find it very difficult to go against what authority says.
4. Before making a decision, I get additional information to make sure I'm prepared.
5. I take a long time to make up my mind because I need to explore the options fully.
6. I often wonder if I'm brave enough to do what must be done.
7. I'm often plagued by doubt.
8. I like to be very sure before acting.
9. Without strict laws it's hard to tell what people might do.
10. I often tend to operate out of a sense of duty and responsibility.
11. I like having limits in which to work.
12. I seem to sense danger and threat more than others do.
13. I tend to take sides and be concerned about whose side people are on.

14. I tend to be aware of and sensitive to contradictions.
15. I prefer to have things scheduled rather than open-ended.
16. Frequently I find myself evaluating others in terms of whether they are a threat to me or not.
17. "Prudence" is a very important virtue for me.
18. I constantly seem to be working against or challenging my fears.
19. I seem to be concerned about defending myself or my position more than other people are.
20. I often fantasize myself in some kind of "hero" role or position.

#7

The compulsion of the SEVEN is avoidance of pain, whether physical or psychological. SEVENS are uncomfortable with persons or situations that are overly serious, laborious or conflictive. To them life should be *fun* and they plan to make it so. They can take even disagreeable things like dieting or penance and make them some kind of fun. In the midst of a family argument they may suddenly interrupt everyone and suggest that they all go out for ice cream!

To avoid the painful SEVENS make plans for some kind of fun in the future. They tend to be optimistic about everything and have a compulsion to overlook whatever is distressing or wrong. Because they want to look at the light side of everything, others experience them as very friendly but rather *superficial* persons.

SEVENS feel a need to flee from whatever is unpleasant even though facing it could bring growth in themselves and in their achievements. This flight from pain can lead them into various forms of self-indulgence. They find it hard to cease doing whatever gives them pleasure. They want to keep on tasting whatever tastes good; to them if some is good, more is better. They approach life this way probably because they grew up in a warm, happy family and then that warmth was taken away. They seem to be always looking for a lost coziness.

SEVENS think of reality as making plans. They look forward to the future with joy because of the plans they have. The present, however, may give them problems which they tend to shirk. Instead of buckling down to the hard work and details of implementing their plans, they make more plans or else seek escape through pleasures. Since they need to have fun in whatever they do, when a task becomes painful, they tend to put it off, even though, once they get absorbed by a project, they probably will complete it. As a result they work in spurts. Once they get enthused about something, they can get much work done and find great satisfaction in their accomplishments. Others may be greatly bothered by their procrastination and say they are not reliable in getting things done in time. SEVENS do tend to be late for just about everything.

Obvious among their good qualities is their ability to find plenty of fun in life. They can bring out a sense of *playfulness* in any family or group. They have ways to brighten up any situation and to get everyone on the bandwagon of "good cheer." Their innate optimism can help others to believe that "everything will work out for the best."

SEVENS enjoy talking, especially telling tales about persons. Though this may tend to be *gossip,* they tell the stories to entertain, rather than to hurt anyone. They are always trying to make everyone happy and even in the midst of distress they can find the bright side of life. As they see it, there are very few things in life that cannot be enjoyed. They smile and laugh frequently and in a childlike way tend to see good in everyone and everything. One of their favorite words is "nice." That is how they want everything to be. They find it easy to like everyone they meet and they try to be very likable themselves.

SEVENS will probably agree with most of the following statements:[13]

1. I seem to be less suspicious of people and their motives than other people are.
2. There are very few things in life which I can't enjoy.
3. Things always work out for the best.
4. I wish other people were more light-hearted about things.
5. I like other people to see me as happy.
6. I usually look on the bright side of things and don't look for the negative side of life.
7. I like almost everyone I meet.
8. I like to tell stories.
9. I like to think of myself as a childlike, playful person.
10. People say I'm often the life of the party.
11. I like to consider the cosmic ramifications of events, the universal importance of everything that happens.
12. My theory is: if something is good, more is better.
13. I don't think it's good to be sad for too long.
14. I like to make things "nice."
15. I like to "savor" life.
16. I tend to be very enthusiastic about the future.
17. I like to cheer people up.
18. Most of the time I avoid getting into really "heavy" issues.
19. I tend to jump from one thing to another rather than go into anything in depth.
20. I remember my childhood as happy.

#8

EIGHTS have a compulsion to avoid any show of weakness. They see life as a power struggle and intend to stay on top. They tend to be intimidating and seem to be looking for a fight. Often they say *no* to people.

Many find it surprising that EIGHTS have little or no remorse in putting people down. As EIGHTS see others, there are many people who are belligerent or hypocritical. EIGHTS intend not to be taken advantage of by such people. They are always ready for confrontation with anyone. They make it their business to unmask the pretenses and injustice of others and in doing so may use expressive or vulgar language. They are quick to pick out the weak side of others and are ready to attack these weaknesses should they be provoked to do so.

EIGHTS have an inner need to pull down all those who consider themselves to be superior. They readily see through people's assertions of power. They are not hesitant to tell another what they want or expect. They find life more satisfying when confronting others because they view reality as having control. They enjoy being strong persons and respect others who are strong. Since they so admire their own *forcefulness,* they quickly lose respect for anyone who seems to compromise on issues. They consider such persons as "wishy-washy." They experience many people as being weak, gullible and half-hearted, and are ready to take on the task of warning them to shape up.

EIGHTS are crusaders for what they see as right and against what they see as wrong. They will join another only if he or she takes a stand against all the others who are wrong. They warn their friends not to let others walk over them. Often EIGHTS see the need for *radical change* in how authority is being exercised and generally are ready to take on the whole power structure, no matter what it is.

Because of the aggressiveness of EIGHTS, others may initially fail to see their lovable qualities. *Courage,* however, is strong love and EIGHTS have an abundance of courage. They are ready to stand up for people no matter who or what may be against them. They are quick to perceive any self-serving attitudes in those above others, whether in the church or in society. Although they may step on many toes, they feel they have reason to do so and are not afraid of getting hurt in the process. Their self-assertion can encourage others of less courage to express their real feelings instead of hiding them because of a fear of rejection. They do not ordinarily fear rejection nor do they care much what others think. They dress to please themselves or to make a statement to others, no matter how others feel about it.

Their ability to get their own way, or at least to get attention from others on some issue, can serve great needs in society or within any group. They are attention-getters and insist on doing what will be noticed. They do not ordinarily hide their dissatisfaction about anything but bring it right out into the open, where it can be dealt with in some fashion.

EIGHTS are to be admired for the *zest* they bring into whatever they do. They have much energy to engage in work, play or in meeting new challenges. They are ready to get involved in things and bring into any situation an intensity of expectations. They see to it that life is not boring.

EIGHTS probably will agree with most of the following statements:[14]

1. I am very good at standing up and fighting for what I want.
2. I sense others' weak points quickly, and I will push them there if I am provoked.
3. I find it easy to express my dissatisfaction with things.
4. I am not afraid to confront other people and I do confront them.
5. I enjoy the exercise of power.
6. I have a sense of where the power resides in a group.
7. I am an aggressive, self-assertive person.
8. I know how to get things done.
9. I have trouble accepting and expressing my tender, gentle, softer, "feminine" side.
10. I get bored easily and like to keep moving.
11. Justice and injustice are key issues for me.
12. I protect people who are under my authority or jurisdiction.
13. I think of myself as being an "earthy" person.
14. Generally, I don't care much for introspection or too much self-analysis.
15. I think of myself as a non-conformist.
16. I don't like to be cornered.
17. I don't like to be told to adjust myself.
18. I think of myself as a hard worker.
19. I have trouble just letting things be.
20. I think other people create their own problems.

#9

NINES have a compulsion to avoid conflict. This is because they experience life with a very low energy level and have the need to avoid tension. Generally they do feel very peaceful within but it is also important to them that conflicts do not arise from without. To them, reality consists in *harmony*. When conflicts do occur they cope with them by denying the importance of the issues causing the conflicts. They will say, "Why get so excited? What's the big deal anyway?" As they see it, most things in life are no big deal.

Probably the way the NINES have of coping with reality was caused by a lack of affection from their parents when they were children, especially from their mothers. Perhaps their parents were simply not affectionate persons or they feared to spoil their children. NINES came to cope with such neglect of love by saying that nothing in life matters anyway. They have a compulsion to deny their own worth and importance. Even in their body language they seem to say, "*I* don't really matter."

As a consequence, their facial expressions and tone of voice will typically be without emphasis or detail. They use colorless words and speak in a monotone or squeaky voice. Their bodily expressions may lack warmth and color. NINES are very *indolent*. They would like to become more alive, but for this they feel they are dependent on external stimuli. Once they do get into some action, they have a poor sense of distinguishing the essential from the peripheral. As a result, they may undertake much activity that has little value or purpose.

NINES are typically great TV watchers. It is important to them, though, that there be no change in the regular programming. An unscheduled news broadcast, for example, is quite upsetting to them merely because it interrupts the regular schedule they expected. Their response may be to sleep through it. Often they give much attention to sports, card playing and collecting knickknacks. They enjoy a *static life* and cling to what is familiar. Since they might experience tensions if they went out to meet new people, they generally tend to avoid going out. They are most content just to keep their old friends and look to them to draw them into more life.

Since NINES avoid becoming excited about anything, they often put off doing things and give some slim excuse for doing so. They tend to be late for appointments or even to forget them entirely. To them time just seems to pass by and they don't know where it goes. It is important to them that things be well scheduled. *Routine* is very satisfying to them because it means an absence of conflict and does not involve making new decisions. When someone asks them to do something more than they are accustomed to do, they don't mind, but it will have to wait until they have completed everything else they were to do.

NINES do have many admirable qualities which are gifts to others. Their very presence can slow people down in a way that is needed by many. Their non-threatening demeanor helps others settle down and become more peaceful. They put a high value on peace and harmony which is important to any group. Their very *availability* to listen to whatever troubles others can bring calmness into an unsettling situation. They are quite *shock-proof* about anything that might be disclosed to them. They rarely give much advice in reply, but they help another see his or her problems in perspective and indicate possible over-reactions to the situation.

NINES are natural arbiters between feuding family members and are very good at bringing about reconciliation. They insist on everyone sitting down and talking out their differences. In such cases they can be very impartial in judgment. To them what is most important is the harmony and peace between persons. Nothing is to be allowed to interfere with that; no other value is as important. To them, *peace is always achievable.*

NINES probably will agree with most of the following statements:[15]

1. Most people get too worked up over things.
2. Most things in life aren't worth getting upset about.
3. I'm almost always peaceful and calm.
4. I like time to just do nothing.
5. I'm an extremely easy-going person.
6. I can't remember the last time I had trouble sleeping.
7. While there are some differences, I feel most people are pretty much the same.
8. Generally, I don't get too enthusiastic about things.
9. There is nothing so urgent that it can't wait until tomorrow.
10. I have a need for outside stimulation to get me going.
11. I hate to waste my energy on anything. I look for energy-saving approaches to things.
12. My attitude is: "I don't let it bother me."
13. I can be a dispassionate arbiter because one side is as good as the other.
14. I hate to be unsettled.
15. I generally follow the line of least resistance.
16. I take pride in being a stable person.
17. I tend to play things down to get other people settled down.
18. I don't think of myself as being all that important.
19. I have trouble listening and paying attention.
20. I agree with this statement: Why stand when you can sit; and why sit when you can lie down.

2. THE ENNEAGRAMIC JESUS

Even though the previous chapter was meant to begin a helpful journey into self, much was found there that could be *very unpleasant.* Admittedly, the fact that each type was described in terms of a dominant compulsion tended to make the descriptions resemble *stereotypes,* or even caricatures, rather than real persons. The intention was to *expose* each compulsion for the blind, prevailing force that it is, in order to attain a new freedom of choice. On the other hand, to focus so much on one's "sin type" could stymie growth by fostering a greater negativity about oneself, or else make one hesitant to accept any classification on the Enneagram. As an *antidote* this second chapter will study the *personality of Jesus* as reflected in the Enneagram types. If Jesus, as presented in the gospels, had these personality types, that makes them much more acceptable to anyone else, despite the weaknesses they portray.

Why should Jesus be thought to have these personality types? Christian theology presents him as assuming in his own person all that needed to be saved. As St. John of Damascus (c. 675-749) stated: "Had there been anything of me not assumed (by the Word of God), it would not have been saved."[16] A practical faith in the incarnation as principal of salvation will insist that Jesus did experience being human *as human nature really is,* including its temptations and weaknesses.

A second question follows: Why would Jesus have *all nine types?* Here the best answer comes from the theory of the Enneagram itself. Each type is characterized by a compulsion, which is a *mistake* in how to live out the good qualities, or "essence," of human nature. Each type has taken a good quality of being human and made it into a compulsion by pushing it to extremes. What was a limited way of being a person is turned into *the ultimate way* of being a person. This is done at the price of failing to become an integrated person. The compulsion is a *sin against wholeness.* It takes a part of personality and pretends it is one's whole self-fulfillment. This shows why Jesus would have had all nine types. By being without sin he was without compulsions. Instead of taking some one quality of being a person and making it his fulfillment, he accepted to live out all the qualities of humanness. By thus avoiding the compulsive behavior of pushing some one quality to an extreme, the distinctive qualities of each Enneagram type could be part of his authentic personality. Because he accepted all nine ways of human personality and lived them without their compulsions, he is able to be a *model* for all personality types in their journey to true freedom.

The method used to explore with the Enneagram the personality of Jesus as presented in the gospels will be to ask *three questions* regarding each of the nine types:

1. How are the good qualities of that type present in Jesus?

2. What is the pitfall, or "trap," of those gifts as found in the compulsion?

3. How did Jesus avoid the "trap" so as to be free of the compulsion?

These three questions lead us into a process of thesis, antithesis and synthesis, characteristic of dialectical thinking. They are themselves a journey into the self of Jesus. To a great extent the data available from the New Testament will have to include an interpretation not only of Jesus' behavior but also a study of what are called "gospel values." The exercise will be like a series of *meditations* on images of Jesus. This will offer a springboard from the Enneagram into Christian spirituality.

#1

Jesus as Idealist

The good qualities of ONES seem to be found in Jesus mainly in his *idealism.* He saw himself as a reformer. To him the world was not the way God intended it to be. Jesus was very concerned that it be set right. He summed up these expectations by saying, "You must therefore be perfect just as your heavenly Father is perfect" (Mt 5:48). Jesus gave himself as the *model of perfection,* even to the extent of saying that no one could "convict" him of sin (Jn 8:46). He worked very hard at setting things right by making his teachings clear to anyone who would listen. He was direct and open with people. To him any kind of deception or conspiracy was of the Evil One. As he said to his accusers, "I have spoken openly for all the world to hear; . . . I have said nothing in secret" (Jn 18:20).

It was important to Jesus to treat everyone equally and with respect. An example of this is shown in the story of the adulterous woman (Jn 8:1-11). The religious leaders are trying to get some evidence of wrong-doing against Jesus so they can have him arrested. They know he is always insisting on forgiveness and compassion, so they drag before him a woman whom they say they have caught in the very act of committing adultery. They point out that in the Bible Moses directed that such a woman should be stoned to death (Dt 22:22-24), and ask him what he has to say about it. Jesus, however, is not interested in discussing theology or exegesis. He is above all aware of the woman and her embarrassment. She has done wrong, yes, but it is not fair to her to be exposed publicly this way. He sees they do not care at all about her; they are only using her to trap him into saying something against the Bible. In actual fact they are much worse sinners than she is because they are in the act of plotting his death. He says, "If there is one of you who has not sinned, let him be the first to throw a stone at her." They all leave one by one beginning with the eldest. When he is left alone with her he says: "Woman, where are they? Has no one condemned you?" She replies, "No one, sir." He then says, "Neither do I condemn you, . . . go away, and don't sin any more." In their characteristic spirit of fairness and equality for all ONES will readily identify with Jesus in this story. Just because the woman's accusers are stronger than she is and have a better public reputation, they should not have an advantage over her in deciding what is just. Even though she has made a moral mistake, she deserves respect for her dignity as a person. She has rights equal to every other human being and it is contrary to those rights for her to be *used* this way.

Pitfalls in Idealism

To have the self-concept of being an idealist can generate much energy in one's life and provide abundant well-deserved self-respect. ONES are hard working, give attention to details and are very perceptive of good and evil. They keep trying to make themselves better and take a lot of time in preparing what they have to do that it be done right. Such idealism, however, can become an *obsession,* leading ONES to be intolerant of the faults of others and very impatient with themselves as well.

In trying to be always perfect, ONES take pains to avoid all anger. Their anger, nevertheless, will still be inside them but pushed down into their subconscious, where it can fester as resentment. It may surface through an irritable tone in their voice. They are constantly bothered by the fact that others are not as they should be and that just about everything should be much better. Because they apply their idealism to themselves a critical inner voice keeps them on their toes in a nagging sort of way. They keep trying to correct themselves rather than accept themselves as imperfect. They also do not accept the imperfections of others but think them obligated to overcome such shortcomings before their behavior will be considered acceptable.

Sometimes ONES find themselves so full of faults that they become moody and despondent. This may arise from seeing that they will never have enough time or energy to get anything done the way it should be. Since they want things always to be in order, any disturbance of this neatness and cleanliness can make them ill at ease and even irritable. For these and other reasons their idealism may cause them to be *fussy* and constantly on edge. They may worry excessively. All this can make it difficult for others to live with them, but especially it makes it *hard for them to live with themselves.*

Becoming More Optimistic

The pitfall of ONES as idealists is too much emphasis on *perfection.* This pitfall, or trap, of perfection is avoided by Jesus in his own idealism by *accepting people as they are.* The perfection of God that Jesus presents as model for everyone actually consists in *compassion* as is shown in the Lukan version of the Sermon on the Mount where Jesus says, "Be compassionate as your Father is compassionate" (Lk 6:36). To make this world better there is need to begin with patience and tolerance for imperfection. There is need to "turn the other cheek" (Lk 6:29), to go the "extra mile" (Mt 5:41), to do good to those who do evil (Lk 6:35). This attitude of compassion is characteristic of God, who "causes his sun to rise on bad men as well as good, and his rain to fall on honest and dishonest men alike" (Mt 5:45). Compassion will result in an *optimism* about human beings and situations, based on the expectation that much good will eventually show itself, even though matters often become better in very small steps. By responding in gentleness to another's pushiness the heart of that person may be touched by the self-awareness that he or she needs to change in attitudes and conduct. Compassion recognizes that the first step for anyone to become better is *to feel loved and accepted as one is.*

ONES need a spirit of optimism as they strive for their own perfection. Since they are human they are subject to a *law of gradual growth* which begins only with self-acceptance. They need to be able to say, "I don't have to be perfect before I am lovable; God made me, God does not make junk." Each person is created by an act of God's love and is meant to be God's unique gift to the world at this point in history. Nobody becomes perfect just by making greater efforts; any real improvement will depend on growth of the God-given power within a person. Primarily this comes through the awareness of being loved unconditionally as manifested in the providential gifts of God and the self-gifts of others.

By taking on such positive attitudes as taught by Jesus, ONES can become much more peaceful. Despite all that is wrong with the world today, there is still much good to be seen and enjoyed. There are even many signs that things are getting better. Many people today are deeply concerned about honesty, justice and universal peace. This is evidence that *God is at work* in human hearts, moving the human race today to desire peace, justice and unity among all persons and nations. The risen Jesus is present throughout the world to overcome disorder, injustice and whatever else is threatening the well-being of the human race. He belongs to the human family and identifies himself with all the issues affecting today's world.

In their daily environment of living and working, ONES can find in Jesus and his teachings an inspiration to keep in mind the *big picture,* rather than to let themselves get bogged down in minutiae. Anything that they can contribute to make things somewhat better around them fits into God's universal plan of love. Jesus identifies himself with his followers and their concern to set things right. His presence, however, is not found in the anxious voice of an inner critic which the ONE may mistakenly think is the "voice of conscience." Instead of listening to that inner critic, ONES need to listen more to what God says through sacred scripture, through others they meet and through the deepest desires of their hearts. ONES need to find God at work also in the aspirations of others, which will often correspond remarkably with the high ideals cherished by ONES. These aspirations, or desires of the heart, can be recognized as flowing from a kind of "underground stream" which is tapped into as a common source of life by those who enter deeply into themselves by contemplation. The ability to experience such contemplation depends on beginning with the attitude of universal compassion which enables a person to accept his or her own mistakes and failures, as well as those of all other persons, as *forgivable.*

ONES benefit greatly by noticing the happy coincidences in their lives. They need to notice how things often worked out just right. This depended not only on their own efforts but on many imperceptible factors. Such instances of *divine providence* often will be not only amazing but also *amusing.* To notice them occur and to remember such past happenings, will help ONES "let go" of their anxieties by relying in a practical way on God's action in their lives.

#2

Jesus Serves Others

TWOS will have little difficulty finding in Jesus a model of their strong motivation to be helpful to others. Jesus sees himself as sent by God to serve others and tells his disciples that if they want to be greater than others they must be servants of all (Mk 10:44). Such service of others includes hugs and all kinds of hospitality, as is shown by Jesus as he holds up and puts his arms around a little child (Mk 10:16). Primarily, of course, service involves *responding to people's real needs.*

Jesus' teachings on being helpful are especially enshrined in his parable of the Good Samaritan (Lk 10:30-37). His followers are to make themselves neighbor to others by taking an initiative in looking for the needs of others and in caring for them out of personal resources. The early Fathers of the Church saw Jesus himself in this parable. He is the Good Samaritan by making himself neighbor to all human beings in need. Such is the way Jesus is presented in all the gospel stories. His heart constantly responds to the needs of others. Sometimes he takes the initiative to help even without the other speaking of his or her need, as is seen, for example, in the miracle of Cana (Jn 12:1-11) and the raising up of the widow's son at Naim (Lk 7:11-15).

Jesus often makes a special point of disregarding Jewish religious laws when in a given case they hinder caring for another's need. He says, "The sabbath was made for man, not man for the sabbath" (Mk 2:27).

Religious laws, and indeed all laws, are to serve real needs of real people. Since the first priority in conscience is to serve the needs of others, laws are to be made to serve persons rather than to make sure that persons serve laws.

TWOS can readily identify with these examples of Jesus' attitude of service, since the image they have of themselves is that of being helpers to others. They place their main concern on the needs of others and devote themselves to doing what they can to help people. They want to be in tune with others' feelings and to be sensitive to each individual. What is most important to TWOS in any time they have with others, even at formal meetings, is to form relationships and to make someone's day brighter.

The Pitfall of Clinging to Others

In their focus on being helpful TWOS operate out of a compulsion to form a relationship which makes the other dependent on them. This is a kind of *clinging* to the other and drawing attention to themselves by finding some way to be of personal service. They simply need to be needed. Even without their realizing it, a *selfishness* creeps into their concern to help. This selfishness desires that the other gives them attention, appreciates them and needs them. A sign that this is so is the way TWOS become quite furious if the other does not take notice of what they have done to please.

Along with this seeking to *win love* from others by serving them and taking pains to please them, TWOS also avoid acknowledging that they themselves have any needs. They say they simply live to make others happy. Actually this attitude makes them dependent on others needing them and having needs that the TWO can satisfy. Should others important to the TWO indicate that they can get along very well without being helped, the TWO will become quite angry and frustrated. The TWO'S very identity and worth is dependent on being needed.

Since ordinary human ideals and especially gospel values stress being of service to others, TWOS will not easily identify their compulsion to be of service for the *vice* it is. Out of what they see as the best of intentions they will go on *manipulating* people to need them and to give them attention because they care for the needs they find in these persons. Actually TWOS are *tying* such persons to them, which is certainly not the proper motivation in loving others.

Acknowledging Personal Needs

It is wise to be aware that real love is not *won* from others, neither from human persons nor from God. Love is always by its very nature a *free gift* from others. People do not love another because that person serves their needs nor because they *need* him or her. They freely *choose* to love or not to love. Love is something they give because they have decided to do so and could have decided otherwise.

According to the gospel message God has freely chosen to love all men and women as sons and daughters. Human beings do not win this love by anything they do for God. This recognition of the *grace* (or gift) of divine love gives all human persons a basis for recognizing they are lovable because of *who* they are rather than for what they do for others. TWOS need to live this kind of faith in God's love. They also will benefit by recognizing that they have needs that God intends for them to take care of out of love for themselves, a love joining the divine love for them. They are to love themselves enough to know that they cannot *always* be thinking only of the needs of others. That would cause them to fall into the trap of using their service of others to win love. A genuine self-love which recognizes and cares for their own needs, can free them from the self-centeredness contained in their saying they live only for others.

Among the personal needs TWOS should take care of by themselves is that of quiet solitude to reflect on their relationships and to allow God's light to penetrate their lives. They will tend to avoid such reflective prayer because deep down inside they want to spend their time *doing for others,* and that includes "doing for God." They are innately reluctant to let God or others do for them. Since meditative prayer is not *doing* anything, it makes them uneasy. Christian faith, however, does center on being cared for by God. The whole story of salvation is based on what God does for human persons. TWOS need to ponder how that true meaning of salvation is affecting their lives, especially as regards how they think of themselves.

In looking to Jesus as a model of helpfulness to others, TWOS should ponder how often Jesus sent people away after working a miracle for them. He avoids tying people to himself through the help he has given them. When the cured demoniac, for example, asks to spend more time with him by joining the company of the disciples, Jesus refuses (Mk 5:18f). Jesus performs miracles for many others and similarly sends them on their way. Often he tells them not to say anything to others about what he has done for them. On the other hand, there are very few instances in the gospels of Jesus working miracles of physical healing for those who follow him as disciples. He is mainly concerned to strengthen them as faithful and courageous witnesses of his attitudes and to communicate his message to others. He seeks to draw them into relating with the Father and the indwelling Spirit the way he does.

Jesus does more than strengthen his disciples and send them on mission for his cause. He also invests much time in being close to them personally and speaks again and again of how much he loves them. He tells them he has a need for them also to love him. A memorable instance of his expressing this need to be loved is when he asked Peter three times, " . . . do you love me . . . ?" (Jn 21:15-17). This is not love based on winning it from them because of what he has done for them; it is based on *communion,* a mutual sharing of hearts. Jesus makes a gift of himself to his disciples. This differs from caring for some need they have. He is first of all a friend to them. An indication they are his friends, he says, is that he has shared with them all he has learned from his father (Jn 15:15). The disciples, in turn, want simply to be with Jesus. Their yearning for communion with him finds new expression after his resurrection when they discover he is with them in a special way whenever they gather in his name (Mt 18:20). This gives them reason to share times of prayer, reflection, meals and social gatherings, simply to be assured of and bathe in his presence. From this experience of communion comes a zeal to share with others what they have discovered of the riches they have been gifted with by the Spirit of Jesus. All this can help TWOS discover the great truth that *real love is ultimately communion rather than acts of service.*

#3

Jesus Works for Success

It can be pointed out to THREES that Jesus is indeed a model for persons who put most of their energy into *achievement.* Jesus lived for his work. He laid out a careful strategy for success, chose persons for special roles in his organization, shared with them his authority and abilities, and held them accountable. He expected of them as much as he expected of himself, which was nothing less than a total dedication to his cause.

Jesus had but one aim in life: building God's Kingdom. He knew he would need a well-disciplined and highly-motivated core group to carry out this goal. Nothing was to be left to chance. After gathering together his disciples, he sent them two by two to all the towns he was planning to enter (Lk 10:1ff). They were given the task of preparing each town for his coming so that people would look forward to his arrival with great expectation and turn out in great crowds to see and hear him.

Jesus was always in charge. This gave great strength to his company of followers and generated a deep loyalty towards him. He knew how to attract women as well as men. St. Luke says the women provided for the whole group "out of their own resources" (Lk 8:3). Jesus was a good salesman; he knew how to express his personality, to awaken admiration and to win followers. He contacted as many people as he could in every way available to him. He made his miracles work for his cause, insisting that the power he exercised not only be noticed but also believed, so as to bring about a favorable reaction to his message.

Despite his immense popularity during most of his public ministry Jesus was careful to spend most of his time with his close followers. He had personally chosen them. They needed considerable *in-service training* for their mission. Jesus did not want his work to be like a flash in the pan. He saw the need for careful organization under the administration of those whom he chose as "The Twelve." These would share his leadership and responsibility over the eventual large numbers of new followers and do so in accordance with his own perspectives and methods. Jesus restricted his own area of work to the relatively small territory of Israel itself, but he was training his apostles to spread the work to the whole world. His own heart expanded with enthusiasm at the thought of all nations coming under the sway of his teachings. For this the groundwork had to be carefully laid. Only then could the world-wide expansion take place with assured success.

As persons with a single-minded goal of achievement for their lives, THREES will find these traits of Jesus' personality an inspiring model. When reminded by others that life is more than achievements, they can point out that Jesus made his work his life, even by sacrificing home and family for it. He would not even let himself take his last breath on the cross until he was satisfied that all his objectives had been fulfilled. Only then could he say, "It is accomplished" (Jn 19:30) and let his spirit leave his body in death.

Pitfalls of Heavy Achievers

To put one's whole investment of life into a single goal has its dangers. Especially it leads to the sacrifice of one's own personal and private life. The value of life itself becomes measured by achievement. Family, intimate friendships and cultural activities tend to be neglected. Because they are totally committed to success, THREES tend to *use* others or else to trample on them. Should a conversation or meeting not seem helpful for what the THREE wants to accomplish, he or she will become very bored and fail to appreciate the value of simply socializing with people and sharing their interests and experiences. Without actually recognizing what is happening to them as persons, THREES will tend to become like machines, repressing their fears, affection and other feelings in order to present themselves as full of enthusiasm for the business at hand. As a consequence they may get out of touch with ordinary life as others live it. They may not notice suffering around them or whatever else is being experienced by others, simply because their own attention is focused on their goals. They may also become quite intolerant of the way their associates seem to waste time talking, come unprepared for meetings or otherwise fail to give their whole souls to the goals of the organization.

When a person's life becomes his or her work virtually all thoughts and feelings are tied to the success being sought. This leaves little room in the heart for what is not directed to the work itself. Many talents may be left untapped, such as those used to entertain others or to express feeling in creative ways. The person ends up identifying self with what she or he *does*, saying, *"I* am a salesman, an executive, an administrator . . . . " Others are forced to relate to the person in terms of his or her *role* rather than simply to a unique person. Should the work of such persons fail or poor health force them into early retirement, they will be at a loss to know what to live for or how to live. Failure could tear them apart and make life utterly meaningless to them.

Accepting Failure

Jesus was a highly motivated person called by God not only to live for a great achievement but also to suffer a *great failure*. This failure of his work began to become apparent at the time of the feeding of the five thousand in the desert. The plotting of the people to make him their political king in response to that miracle (Jn 6:15) showed that despite all his teaching they still did not understand his real values. He had simply failed to become their leader. As a result he left Galilee and spent most of the rest of his life in Judea, especially in Jerusalem itself, where he openly confronted the established religious leaders. His failure in Galilee had not torn him apart; instead, he reacted by becoming more assertive in a public way. He had also learned to be ready for further failures in attracting people to his values.

Jesus can be a model for THREES to accept what they most fear, namely, *failure.* Instead of trying to succeed *at all costs,* they can let themselves be known as they really are, even if that means others will turn away from them and their causes. Because of their determination to succeed they are tempted to compromise themselves, deceiving not only others but themselves as well. Jesus exemplifies the importance of *not sacrificing personal integrity* for the sake of achieving one's goals. Jesus could have acted otherwise. He could have gone along with the popular movement to make him king of Israel. He could have said that by becoming king he would have more power to influence bringing about the Kingdom of God. This, however, would have been giving in to the temptation of the Evil One, as he had told his disciples concerning his experiences in the desert. It would amount to worship of the Devil (Mk 4:5-8). Thereby as Messiah he would *misuse* the power given him by God.

THREES need to keep in mind that *the end does not justify the means.* The great value accorded success by society today tends to obscure this great moral principle. Often, waging war is considered a means to peace, violence is exercised to protect human rights, and deception and telling lies are used to achieve national security. Jesus taught people not to hide their real intentions by deceptive tactics. He insisted on truthfulness even at the risk of failing in one's goals and plans. His own death on the cross showed he lived out that teaching. As he looked down from the cross and saw the failure of practically all he had worked for, he let it all go and put his own spirit in the hands of his father (Lk 23:46). His death meant he would not sacrifice any of his values for the sake of his work being accepted by others.

#4

Jesus is Sensitive

FOURS will readily see Jesus as the patron of misunderstood people. He frequently complained to his disciples that even they did not understand him. A reason for this feeling of being misunderstood was his very deep *sensitivity*. His heart felt the vibrations of others' emotions and especially their tragedies and sorrows.

The gospel stories are filled with signs of Jesus' great compassion, such as his grief at seeing the widow of Naim burying her only son (Jn 11:35), his tears joining those of his friends because Lazarus had died (Jn 11:35), and his healing the woman who had been bent over with a stiff back for eighteen years (Lk 13:10-17). In the latter case he was exasperated by the religious leaders arguing that she should not have been healed because that was doing work on the sabbath. Jesus said they had more feeling for an *ox* than for the woman!

The great sensitivity of Jesus also gave him a flair for the symbolic and dramatic as is characteristic of FOURS. He often had a grand way of fulfilling the scriptures, such as by saying his crucifixion would be like Moses' raising up the bronze serpent in the desert

(Jn 8:13f) and by riding an ass into the city of Jerusalem to be hailed as the Son of David (Mt 21:6-8). He saw the *drabness* and routine of the Jewish religion in which he had been brought up, its ponderous attachment to *law* as the way to reach God and its neglect of persons "unclean" because they had leprosy, despicable because they had fallen into prostitution, or lacking a voice in society because they were women. He related well with sensitive people, those who would weep buckets over their sins, as did the prostitute in Simon the Pharisee's house (Lk 7:36:50), or who would argue with him that he should give at least a few "crumbs" of help to the poor pagans (Mk 7:24:30). Jesus did not mind getting a bad reputation from his association with persons who did not keep the Jewish law. They too had hearts and he was always ready to reach out to the human heart.

Jesus' male disciples had grown up in a religion of law rather than of the heart. This meant that God's word was much more law than love. As a consequence they continually misunderstood Jesus in the substance of what he taught which was founded on *sensitivity.* An instance of their lack of sensitivity is their complaint about the woman of Bethany pouring luxurious perfume over Jesus' head (Mt 26:6-13). This, they say, is a "waste!" Could not the perfume instead have been sold and the money given to the poor? Their reaction makes Jesus feel very misunderstood. They don't even suspect how heavy his heart is! Very soon he must die, yet they begrudge him this gesture of love! He rises up to defend the woman's action, saying that what she has just done for him will be announced to the whole world until the end of time!

During the passion Jesus was saddened by the way his disciples failed to understand what it meant for him not only to face the failure of his life work but also to experience the amazing hatred of all who held him prisoner. He tried to show them at the Last Supper that he suffered greatly just from having to leave them. Later, in his hour of anguish at Gethsemani when his whole soul became like jelly, his three favorite disciples, Peter, James and John fell asleep only a few yards away while Jesus himself was *"sweating blood"* (Mt 26:36-40; Lk 22:44).

The Pitfall of Melancholy

The pitfall of FOURS is melancholy. They not only are hypersensitive to any hurts or misfortunes, but also they keep recalling such tragedies in the memory again and again. The drama of their lives, especially its sad parts, is viewed as very significant. They feel special because they have been overlooked or abandoned by others or simply not appreciated.

They also tend to be *snobbish*. They take pride in their superior good taste and in the superior way they understand joys and sorrows. They tend to "put on" a style of personality, even practising beforehand how they will express themselves to others. They are always seeking to have the "right" style, that which will demonstrate their uniqueness. They also tend to think others are lacking in style and refinement. All this makes them seem a bit *unreal* as persons, as though they display more feeling than is actually in the heart.

FOURS are inclined to indulge in self-pity to

draw attention to themselves as almost *overwhelmed* by tragic events. They feel others do not understand all they have gone through. Despite all the *sighs* they heave, they probably will not let another really know their heart since they don't believe anyone can understand them anyway. This makes it difficult to get really close to a FOUR as an intimate friend.

Avoiding Self-pity

Like FOURS, Jesus was a "man of sorrows" but he carefully avoided melancholy and self-pity. He did not portray himself as ultimately *a tragic figure,* but instead as on the way to becoming the triumphant Son of Man. He told his disciples of his coming passion and death and, at the same time, spoke of his resurrection from the dead (Mk 8:31f). He did yearn for his death but as a "baptism" giving him new powers of salvation for the world which would be shared with his followers. He was going through his passion and death for others. Though the "prince of this world" would seem to triumph (Jn 14:30), it would be a short-lived victory and the end result would be a victory of Jesus over sin and death.

Jesus' disciples, however, refused to listen whenever he sought to convey to them his thoughts about going through death for the sake of resurrection. They did not want to hear of the Kingdom of God coming through his death. Peter even took Jesus aside and said, "This must not happen to you." (Mt 16:22) as though the disciples could prevent Jesus' enemies from harming him. Jesus reacted in anger to Peter's remonstrance because what Peter had said was directly contrary to God's design as Jesus saw it. He then turned to all his disciples and told them they must be ready to suffer as he would suffer (Mt 16:23-26). Jesus is avoiding being a lone tragic figure. All his disciples, in seeking to bring about the Kingdom of God in this world, are to see themselves like Jesus in being ready to suffer even the loss of their lives for its attainment.

As Jesus became more aware of the growing conspiracy against him, he did not run into hiding with his friends, but instead presented himself even more openly to the public. He went down to Jerusalem to face those conspiring against him. He engaged them in discussion and let them know him personally. Rather than brooding about the way others were against him and how they failed to see his innocence and goodness, he sought to meet people as long as he was free to move about (Jn 12:35f). If he could not touch their *hearts* by miracles of healing, then at least he would try to touch their *minds* by logic. Jesus was not a *milquetoast* but a real man. Along with his other gifts he had the acute mind of a scholar even though he had not studied in any of the elite schools. As his enemies gathered their forces against him, he reacted by increasing his activity of teaching in the temple area, right in the center of Jerusalem.

The sadness and self-pity characteristic of FOURS often leads them to inactivity and even to *clinging to another* for understanding and protection in a desperate sort of way. As Jesus' own mental suffering increased, he did just the opposite. He became more active and less surrounded by his chosen disciples. Instead of leaning on them for support in the last days before his arrest and death, he tried to support them and prepare them for the coming trial. He saw himself as a shepherd being struck down with the consequence that they, his sheep, would be scattered (Mk 14:27). He insisted they were to strengthen one another, especially by loving one another as he had loved them (Jn 13:33-35), after they had lost his physical presence (Lk 22:32).

Jesus left his apostles a share of his own power to forgive, heal and bring new life to others. They were to exercise these powers through symbolic gestures and words such as he had used. They were never to forget how Jesus had healed people by putting his finger into their deaf ears (Mk 7:33), making mud with his saliva and dabbing it on their blind eyes (Jn 9:6) or letting power from his body go out to a woman when she touched the hem of his garment (Lk 8:44). He wanted them to follow his example in putting feeling and creativity into religion. Thereby his own heart could be put into a world that often seems to have lost its heart.

#5

Jesus Loves Wisdom

FIVES can readily identify with Jesus in his insistence that one's life be built on wisdom. He probably would agree with Socrates' aphorism that "the unexamined life is not worth living." Jesus was a man who thought things out personally with the light God put into his heart. He spent much time alone in prayer and reflection and then shared what he had learned with his followers (Jn 15:15). He built his own life on the truth he discovered in life through "the signs of the times" (Lk 12:56) and invited others also to do so. He taught that to be ready to enter God's Kingdom it was not sufficient just to accept doctrine handed down by others; one also needed to gain insight into the meaning God was placing in events at the present time in history.

As Jesus reflected on his experiences with people, he saw through nonsense, pretense and falsehood in the way they lived. He saw what was needed in their religion was to establish some *priorities* on what was more important in God's eyes as distinct from what was less important. Much of this was summed up in Matthew's gospel in the Sermon on the Mount (Mt 5-7) and Jesus presented it to his disciples as a *solid rock of wisdom* on which to build their lives (Mt 7:24). Those who listened to him found a freshness in his teaching because he spoke out of his own life and convictions. They said he spoke with authority and not like the other religious teachers who were always citing various opinions (Mt 7:29). He challenged his adversaries to come to know the truth through him. That truth, he said, would make them free (Jn 8:31f).

Jesus was like a FIVE also in the way he summed up his insights in pithy statements, such as "Do not judge, and you will not be judged" (Mt 7:1), "Many who are first will be last, and the last first" (Mk 10:31), and "my yoke is easy and my burden light" (Mt 11:30). He loved symbols and analogies and often had people think in images, as when he told his disciples to avoid the "yeast" of the Pharisees (Mk 8:15), to keep "their loins girt," ready for the final coming (Lk 12:35) and to recognize that his "food" was to do the will of God (Jn 4:34). Jesus invented original ways of communicating the truths he had discovered in his reflection and promised that his followers would also experience a well-spring of creativity within themselves, overflowing for the benefit of many (Jn 7:37). Truly Jesus was a man of wisdom, a *guru* who initiated his disciples into a way of discovering truth through which God could teach them directly in their hearts.

The Trap of Aloofness

In their search for understanding through private study and reflection, FIVES tend to fall into the trap of *aloofness*. They are wary of commitment to groups and social events, and even tend to be cynical about people whom they see as speaking in platitudes and never engaging in any hard logic or real study. To seek wisdom requires much time spent on one's own study projects, and FIVES tend to be stingy in giving up that time to be with others. FIVES often say they do not like parties because they find them shallow and boring. Even when at a social gathering they may be preoccupied with their own thoughts and thus present a rather indifferent, or even cold, exterior. Since they give the impression of knowing more than they say, others may resent their quietness and reserve.

FIVES are not always quiet. When given the occasion to do so they give a very clear presentation of what they have been thinking about. They like to unfold it as a small treatise on the subject with the material summed up under a number of headings for utmost clarity. As they go on and on, others become nervous or simply stop listening. When FIVES experience this evidence of not being appreciated for what they have to say, they tend to retreat all the more into their heads where they are always at home with their thoughts anyway.

A Thinker Who Cares

Despite Jesus' great penchant for personal reflection, he carefully avoided the trap of the FIVE. He began his ministry by living with a band of close friends with whom he shared all that God revealed in his heart (Jn 15:15). Although he often went apart from them to lonely places, when they intruded into his solitude Jesus seems not to have shown any annoyance (Mk 1:35-38), probably because he was so grateful to have them with him as loyal disciples.

He did not try to share with them everything all at once. There was a gradual, step-by-step approach in his pedagogy. This is illustrated by his instruction on love of neighbor which was at the heart of his gospel message. First Jesus pointed out that already in the Old Testament all the commandments boil down to two, namely, love of God and love of neighbor (Lk 10:25-28). Then Jesus said that the commandment of love of neighbor is "similar" to that of love of God (Mt 22:39), thereby suggesting that in order to love God one must love neighbor. After that Jesus has his disciples expand their awareness concerning who is the neighbor they are to love, *viz.*, anyone of the human race who is in need. They are told to make themselves neighbor, to go out looking for the needy (Lk 10:30-37). Eventually the disciples are shown that by serving the needs of others they are actually loving Jesus himself, and that this is the criterion for being among the just on the last day (Mt 25:31-46). Just before he died Jesus added to his teaching on love of neighbor what he called his "new commandment," that they love one another as he had loved them, and that by the observance of this commandment they would be known as his disciples (Jn 13:34f). Finally Jesus prays that all his followers become one as he and Abba are one. Through this unity among believers in truth and love, the world, he says, will come to believe that he was sent by God (Jn 17:20-23). As the disciples listened to Jesus unfold this teaching they learned it well. After the resurrection the apostolic church put in the forefront of its concerns Jesus' teachings on love of neighbor (Cf 1 Th 3:12f).

Jesus especially avoided presenting a treatise of doctrine to the people he taught in the streets and synagogues. To them he usually told stories in the form of parables. It certainly must have been painful for him to leave it to his listeners to discover for themselves the point he was making and then to apply it to their lives. He had to adapt himself, however, in order to get them to listen to him at all. People were not likely to take notes but they would remember a story, and as they thought about it later and repeated it to others they might discover the wisdom within it. He expected his disciples, however, to grasp the meaning of the parables right away. When they do not understand Jesus is patently disappointed with them (Mt 13:14-16). Being a wise man himself he wants them to learn wisdom. He is always patient, though. And his great adaptability as a teacher who speaks simply, and even in a folksy way, stands out graphically when compared with St. Paul, who did not hesitate to begin a letter with a synthesis of God's plan over all creation from the beginning to the end of time (Eph 1)!

Because Jesus was a thinker who really cared for people and loved them deeply however they were, he avoided the aloofness and cynicism typical of the FIVE. He was always ready to repeat his explanations. He encouraged others to draw him out with questions. He took kindly and seriously questions that must have seemed stupid to him, such as at the ascension when he was asked if he was about to restore the kingdom to Israel (Ac 1:6). The average FIVE would have gone up into the clouds with a huff at that one, making it a very unpleasant scene of departure. Jesus, however, saw the question as an opportunity to communicate something. On an earlier occasion when he talked with the woman at the well, he responded on a deeper level to each of the woman's comments or questions, even though some of them were completely inane. By keeping with her in dialogue, which certainly must have tried his patience, he eventually moved her to express her faith in the Messiah and then to discover he was that Messiah (Jn 4:7-26).

It may be surprising that in the gospels there is often more concentration on the miracles Jesus worked than on the content of his teaching. The evangelist will say, "While Jesus was teaching, a certain person came up . . . ," and then go on to relate a miracle story. What is happening here is that the *teaching* is indeed being presented. God's intervention in people's lives is to be discovered through events that happen. The wise person is not one who collects knowledge but one who *discovers truth*. To become wise is to enter into a *process* of contact with events. Jesus came with a gift of *how to be wise*. With that gift people can sort things out for themselves in an on-going way. To live wisely means to be present to each person and event, ready to discover God's truth and love being disclosed as gift. Life itself is the best teacher. Underlying whatever happens is the hand of God outstretched in a "diaphanous experience", one can *see through* the event to a deeper reality of Truth. A whole pattern of God's graces are to be discovered in one's life, each like a door opening into a larger room where one can live more freely and fully. Such entering into the Kingdom of God is like finding a new world within the present one. It demands, though, that a person be a *participant* in the mystery of life and not merely an observer.

Such true wisdom calls people to be ready with the "loins girt" to live in the present moment with the desire to see God's gifts coming to them, gifts which teach and correct, enliven anad strengthen, surprise and comfort. This tells FIVES that if they want to be truly wise they must avoid aloofness. The Kingdom of God arrives in the present. Not to be involved and committed to what happens outside oneself is to risk ultimately becoming a fool. It will entail the missing of God's wisdom being unfolded in events which can be known only by personal involvement with them.

#6

Jesus is Loyal

SIXES, who typically insist on loyalty to a group, whether it be family, church or business organization, can find a model of loyalty in Jesus. All the energy of his public life went into contributing what he could to build up the quality of life in his religion and among his people. His devotion knew no bounds, even to the giving up of his life. As Caiphas said, not without irony, it was better for one man to die than for the whole nation to perish. As the evangelist explained the statement, Jesus died to bring into unity the scattered children of God (Jn 11:49-52).

Jesus' dedication to people was always governed by his loyalty to God, whose promised gift he was to the Chosen People, the Jews. He accepted his life as the fulfillment of the scriptures, with all the demands that made on him. He liked to think of himself simply as the faithful servant of God. As he said, he had come not to be served, but to serve, "and to give his life as a ransom for many" (Mk 10:45). Although his heart opened out to the whole world of nations, he remained faithful to being *God's gift to Israel.* It was to his apostles that he entrusted the mission to the Gentiles. When he heard that Greeks were interested in talking with him, he did not even consider fleeing with them to escape his impending arrest; instead, he saw it as a sign that the time had arrived to give himself over to death (Jn 12:20-33), since he knew from the scriptures that salvation was to come to the Gentiles only through his death as a sacrifice to God.

Jesus was faithful not only to the scriptures but also to the whole Jewish law. He stated that no one could convict him of any sin (Jn 8:46) and, try as they might, those who had him arrested could find no evidence of his guilt to present before the Sanhedrin. They had to rely on false witnesses who twisted Jesus' words to say that he would destroy the temple (Mk 14:58), that he opposed paying taxes to Caesar and that he called himself a king (Lk 23:2).

Jesus expressed a very special loyalty to those closest to him. Out of dedication to his chosen disciples he had left his home, his carpenter shop and all his possessions in order to spend all his time with them. He said it was for them that he was giving up his life:

A man can have no greater love than to lay down his life for his friends. You are my friends . . . (Jn 15:13f)

As he hung from the cross and saw his mother standing there, out of a son's loyalty to her he asked his favorite disciple, John, to take his place in being her son after he was gone (Jn 19:25-27). Only then, having fulfilled all his obligations, could he allow himself to die (Jn 19:30).

Legalism and Self-righteousness

In their great insistence on loyalty SIXES often slip into the trap of *legalism*. They tend to make the observance of laws an end in itself rather than a means to an end. This is because they experience life as the fulfillment of *demands*. They perceive morality and religion to be focused on the observance of laws. Even a person's relationship with God tends to be judged by the outward observance of laws and regulations.

The reason for making religion center on the outward observance of laws is *security*. By outward observance a person can claim to be under God's blessing and assured of salvation. Such legalism tends to lead to another pitfall, that of *self-righteousness*. Since the external observance of laws gives security to the SIX, any deviance from these obligations undermines that security. As a result, the SIX is reluctant to admit any such deviance. Should others suggest to the SIX some neglect of obligations, some slippage in the standards of responsibility so much insisted upon, he or she will deny this or else point out more serious delinquencies in others.

Along with the strict observance of written laws, SIXES may find security by obeying someone in authority. Should it be difficult in a given instance to decide what to do, SIXES typically prefer the answer to come from an external authority. By obeying that person's decision the SIX feels sure he or she is doing what is right. To SIXES it seems that God himself could not charge them with doing the wrong thing as long as they are being obedient to their superior.

The Spirit of the Law

Jesus avoided the trap of seeking ultimate security from external observance of law. The New Testament shows that laws are only means to right relationship with God; this is to follow the "spirit of the law" rather than the "letter of the law." Such a distinction is of fundamental importance to St. Paul. He says that Christ set us free from *slavery to the law,* and Christ meant us to remain free (Gal. 5:1). To make rigid observance of law the final arbiter of one's relationship with God makes law an end in itself. Such observance of law can actually be a grave obstacle to entering into right relationship with God at all. It is a kind of self-salvation that says one is saved by observance of law rather than by the grace of God. As St. Paul states: "If the law can justify us, there is no point in the death of Christ" (Gal 2:21).

What then does it mean to live by the "spirit of the law" rather than the "letter of the law"? To live by the letter of the law is to make observance of law *that which determines one's relationship with God.* On the other hand, to live by the spirit of the law is to recognize that observance of law, even though important, is not that which *causes* right relationship with God. SIXES need to think about this because they have a compulsion to interpret life in terms of responding to demands made on them and to judge others in accordance with these demands. It is true that St. Paul's struggle to explain the "cause of justification," that which brings a person into union with God, is one of the most difficult points of Christian teaching. This difficulty, however, stems in large part from the fact that so many Christians have wanted to cast religion and morality into the mold of the SIX'S viewpoint on life. Legalism, of course, will seem the more logical viewpoint for anyone who views God primarily as a lawgiver. Jesus, however, came to reveal how God really is, namely, Abba, a loving parent.

To hold to the spirit of the law rather than to the letter of the law corrects two errors. One is an *error in morality;* the other an *error in religion.*

When law is made an end in itself there is an *error in morality* from the fact that all laws then tend to have the same importance because the breaking of any law is an *act of disobedience to the lawgiver.* Jesus, however, taught that not all laws are of equal importance. He insisted on certain priorities regarding laws, with love of God and love of neighbor always the primary consideration. He charged that the Pharisees lacked that proper ordering in their observance of religious and moral laws. He said they neglected the "weightier" matters of the law, such as justice, mercy and sincerity, while observing minute details of the law, such as tithing on the spices of their gardens. He did not say they should neglect any of the laws but that in observing laws they must be sure to put in first place these more important obligations (Mt 23:23). They make the mistake, he says, of "Straining out gnats and swallowing camels" (Mt 23:24). St. Paul followed Jesus' insistence on the primacy of love. As St. Paul says, "the whole of the Law is summarized in a single command: Love your neighbor as yourself" (Gal 5:14).

When the observance of law is made an end in itself there is also an *error in religion.* Religion is about salvation seen in terms of a right relationship with God, indeed, a *union with God.* The word "religion" stems from the Latin word *religare,* which is also the root for the word "rely." Religion involves *relying on God,* which means having a relationship with the Almighty based on a confident dependence. To cling to observance of law as assuring a right relationship with God is, in fact, to make an absolute of the external observance of laws. According to the New Testament people are to rely on God because divine love is revealed in and through Jesus, not because they are faithful observers of laws. It is Jesus' love that "causes" God to save people through an act of divine adoption. As St. Paul states, "God sent his Son, born of a woman, born a subject of the Law, to redeem the subjects of the Law and to enable us to be adopted as sons" (Gal 4:4f). St. Paul goes on to say that since we are sons (and daughters) we are destined for salvation because God will give us what properly is the inheritance of the Son (Gal 4:6f).

The message of salvation corrects the great mistake SIXES make concerning the demands of law. Salvation is not based on the actions a person performs to carry out responsibilities. It is based on something preceding that, namely, being re-born as a son or daughter of God. A person can be in right relationship with God only by acknowledging this bond with God as Abba and responding with the love and dedication befitting a filial relationship. This includes imitating God in one's attitude and behavior towards others by being compassionate, forgiving, just and kind. The obeying of laws remains important, but must be seen only as a way to live out the commandments of love of God and love of neighbor. The actual cause of salvation is God's act of divine adoption which initiates a bonding with God.

#7

Jesus is Optimistic

SEVENS appreciate the fact that Jesus knew how to have fun with his friends. He surprised his apostles with a beach party after the post-resurrection miraculous catch of fish (Jn 21). The men undoubtedly expected a scolding after Jesus caught them fishing instead of doing their work as missionaries. Jesus is in a sense correcting them but he does it by entering into their sport. After they tell him they have caught nothing all night he points out where to throw out their nets to catch some. That the gospel writer remembers the exact number of fish, *viz.,* one hundred fifty three, shows that before the event was written down it had been a fish story told again and again to fascinated audiences of early Christians. To be invited to add some of *their* fish to the ones Jesus already had cooking in the pan was a hint they were to join their efforts with those of Jesus "to catch men" (Mk 1:12). Certainly it was an enjoyable way for Jesus to make a point.

Jesus liked to have a good time with people. His adversaries accused him of enjoying wine and not being as ascetical as a prophet should be, as exemplified especially by John the Baptist (Mt 11:18f). Jesus' response was that being with him was like being guests at a wedding party; it was not a time to be sad (Mt 9:15). Jesus had shown this attitude earlier in the miracle at Cana. His changing into choice wine the water in six stone jars, with each jar holding twenty to thirty gallons, was meant as a sign of the Kingdom of God already made present in the person and actions of

Jesus (Jn 2:1-11). It recalled Old Testament pro-
phecies that a sign of the Messiah would be to have an
abundance of food and wine, as stated, for example,
in Isaiah 25:6

*On this mountain Yahweh Sabaoth will prepare for all peoples a
banquet of rich food, a banquet of fine wines of food rich and
juicy, of fine strained wines.*

Jesus' personality had no difficulty in enjoying such
signs of the Kingdom of God. He gladly added to the
Cana party an over-abundance of the best wine. He
liked to say that heaven will be like an everlasting wedding feast (Mt 22:2), and he did not hesitate to engage
in such an anticipation of heaven.

    Such "messianic abundance" was also shown by
the meal he gave to the five thousand in the desert
through a multiplication of five loaves of bread and
two fish (Mk 6:35-44). Jesus wanted his disciples to see
the *sign* in this from the twelve baskets of leftovers
(Mk 8:19-21). Instead of worrying about not having
provided enough food for their journey, they should
see that such a sign of God's providence gives them
reason to trust there will always be enough. This
abundance is also indicated by the institution of the
eucharist as a sign of what Jesus' death would provide
for his followers. There will be a never-ending
nourishment from the human presence of Jesus and
this will ensure his followers that they will attain the
joy of eternal life (Jn 6:54). That a *banquet* of food
and drink should be the principal way Christians have
of thanking God for the gift of salvation in Jesus is
itself the kind of worship that stresses *enjoyment*
together rather than self-abnegation.

SEVENS can easily relate to Jesus as a person whose heart yearned for the good things to come as a result of God's promises. Jesus showed, in fact, that the Kingdom of God is not only yet to come but is already *here*, "at hand," in a real, though incomplete way. The Kingdom consists in the enjoyment together of the gifts of God to believers. Unless a person knows how to enjoy life, how could such preaching of the Kingdom by Jesus ever have much appeal?

The Problem of Pain

Simply because they are such fun-loving persons, SEVENS have a real problem with *pain*. Any kind of discomfort may seem to them a great evil to avoid. To have things always pleasant and "nice," they try to avoid all conflict. They keep "sweeping dirt under the rug" to have a veneer of "peace" over everything. They may also be great procrastinators. Rather than buckle down to do what is unpleasant they put it off. Instead of completing what they have already planned to do they go off making more plans. When things pile up or their plans fail to work out they may become sulky and irritable. To escape from such negative feelings they may over-indulge in whatever pleasures they can find.

Finding Security in the Present Moment

To have such a great need for pleasure is indeed a *trap* to the personality. SEVENS are trying to find more security in fun that it can ever provide. Jesus' own approach to the problem of pain was much more realistic. He could always find security *in the present moment* no matter how he felt, because, as both he and John the Baptist preached, "the kingdom of heaven is close at hand" (Mt 3:1; 4:17). This was the core message because it was *the core experience* of the Kingdom of God. Although the Kingdom was indeed something to be more enjoyed in the future than in the present, the only way the future enjoyment would come about was to be alert and present to the moment at hand. This was because the Kingdom was as a seed that grows after it is planted in the present moment. It is true that the present moment may be painful or dark or menacing, but whatever pain or trouble there is in the present moment is a sign and preparation for the joyful future planned by God. Before joy there is often sadness, just as a seed "dies" before it produces a harvest (Jn 12:24), and a mother endures labor pains before she has the joy of a baby born into the world (Jn 16:21). Whatever the pain of the present moment it is to be much less than the joy to follow. As St. Paul says, when the present suffering has passed away it will seem as nothing in comparison with the "weight" of eternal glory destined for us (2 Cor 4:17).

It is also unrealistic for SEVENS to expect everything to be fun. Surely it is not that important to avoid whatever is painful. A person may find reasons to say it is fun to change a baby's diapers, but why not say that real love does not mind doing what is not all that pleasant? The point is, *pain is not necessarily to be avoided.* Seen as a *price* to be paid for some good, it ceases to be a great evil. Jesus went through his own suffering and death with great hope which gave him courage and patience. He was suffering *for something;* it was his way of "giving birth." He tells his apostles that their present sadness, too, is like labor pain (Jn 16:20-22). Trying to avoid discomforts by some kind of escape may cause one to miss the joy that painstaking creativity can bring about.

St. Paul sees all creation now groaning in labor pains, yearning for its deliverance from evil (Rm 8:18-22). The risen presence of Jesus which fills the whole universe (Eph 4:10), assures creation of a new birth. The "groaning" needs to be there, for the coming of a glorious future involves the cross of suffering. Evil needs to be overcome by patience and endurance. Every difficulty patiently endured is a *seed* that will eventually prepare a great harvest, that of everlasting happiness. All longing for a better life, all feelings of lack or emptiness, can be taken into a cosmic process for the restoration of Paradise. This is made possible through the presence of the risen Jesus within that cosmic process. What was once lost is to be restored, but in God's good time, and through the paschal mystery of death and resurrection. Meanwhile the followers of Jesus are always to have their answer ready for people who ask them the reason for the hope they have (1 Pet 3:15). Troubles themselves can produce patient endurance, which brings God's approval and is a cause to live in hopeful expectation (Rm 5:3-4).

#8

Jesus Confronts Injustice

EIGHTS will readily relate to Jesus as a *strong person*. An outstanding example of his strength is his dealing with the money-changers in the temple (Jn 2:13-17).[17] Jesus decides to confront head on the disgrace of cheating the poor in the sacred precincts. That a rope in his hand was sufficient to cause all the merchants to flee suggests they knew they were doing wrong. It was, of course, what a prophet in Israel might do, but it also shows that Jesus was *fearless*. The disciples were surprised of the anger he displayed, but explained it as his zeal for the rights of God.

Another episode showing Jesus' prophetic confrontation of official injustice and hypocrisy is seen in his stern preaching against the scribes and Pharisees in Matthew 23. They say he has insulted them. Jesus certainly does not mince any words as he calls them not only hypocrites but also "white-washed sepulchers," "blind guides," and a "brood of vipers." He does not hesitate to take them all on as he defends justice and truth. He has it out with them because he has a great distaste for their playing roles and pretending to be just and holy. They were in a position of being image-setters for the Jewish religion modeling what God willed and what God was like, yet they made their authority a means to keep God's will from being done. As a class apart from the ordinary people they used their education and wealth for their own self-aggrandizement and conspired to get rid of Jesus whom they correctly saw as a threat to all that they had attained. Jesus continually seeks to become their savior too, by trying to lead them to repentance. He fails just as John the Baptist had earlier failed (Mt 3:7ff). These men deny any need to repent, while at the same time they are planning to have Jesus put to death. They will even go to the extent of bribing one of Jesus' own disciples to get him arrested, and they call on false witnesses during his trial to get him convicted. When the soldiers report his empty tomb on Easter Sunday, they are bribed to say that the body was stolen while they were asleep (Mt 28:12f)!

Jesus did not remain silent about the evil he saw in his society even though he did not have the political power to do much about it. He did not fear being killed for speaking up. He firmly believed that those responsible for injustice should be confronted; otherwise they would simply go on oppressing others for their own advantage and be blind to their own sinfulness. He believed injustice should be exposed for what it is; to let it remain hidden is to play into the hands of those who conspire to evil. As St. Paul says, the children of light are to bring all things into light; evil doers hate the light and flee from it, for much of their power over others is through deception and trickery (Eph 5:11-13).

Jesus, with his strong sense of justice and readiness to challenge the powers that be, is a model for EIGHTS. Like all EIGHTS, Jesus saw through those who use violence to exert their influence or defend their position. He saw they were actually acting out of weakness. True strength is possessed by persons who, as Jesus says, do not fear those who can kill the body but cannot dispose of the soul (Mt 10:28). Jesus calls on his followers *not to compromise their consciences,* even at the cost of suffering and death.

Controversial but not Cantankerous

EIGHTS have a gift in their boldness to confront injustice. Their pitfall is to go around looking for a fight. They are *cantankerous,* asserting themselves at the expense of others. They like to be not only against others but also *over others.* Such authoritarianism aids them in being in control. As a result, others often find it difficult to relate to them.

Jesus himself reacted to the sinful behavior of others in many different ways and certainly not always by confrontation. He defended the adulterous woman while doodling in the sand (Jn 8:3-11), invited himself as a friend into the home of the wealthy tax collector, Zachaeus (Lk 19:1-10), and declined to continue John the Baptist's confrontation with King Herod after John was beheaded. Even in his attacks on the scribes and Pharisees it could be argued that Jesus was confronting them as a *class* with vested interests, what today would be called an "unjust structure," rather than denouncing them as individuals.

Being Vulnerable

Jesus' role as a prophet cannot be understood without seeing how he allowed himself to be *vulnerable.* This is especially evident in his passion and death. He said he had the power to prevent his arrest and crucifixion (Mt 26:53). In the Garden of Gethsemani the soldiers coming to seize him fell to the ground when he said, "I am he" (Jn 18:6), as though paralyzed by the power of his word and presence. To their violence, however, Jesus offered no counterviolence. As he told Peter, "all who draw the sword will die by the sword" (Mt 26:52).

Jesus saw real strength in non-violence, for God works through one's own gentleness in the face of oppression by others. Jesus expressed this truth at the time he drove the money-changers from the temple when he said that if they destroyed the temple of his body he would raise it up again (Jn 2:19). He viewed the utter weakness and nakedness shown in his crucifixion as giving him the power to heal the world, like the bronze serpent lifted up on a pole by Moses in the desert (Jn 3:13f). The sight of his crucifixion was the occasion for many of his enemies to see that they were in the wrong.[18] Had Jesus simply used his power to confront them while protecting himself from harm they surely would have remained convinced they were in the right.

In his instruction to his disciples on being witnesses before the world, Jesus inculcates in them both a fearlessness in speaking out and a willingness to suffer the consequences without resisting by counterviolence. In pondering Jesus' teachings on non-violence, EIGHTS should ask whether they confront injustice in ways that could lead another to repent, or if they simply seek to *prevail* over those who do wrong.

#9

Jesus is Patient

NINES can appreciate the *patience* of Jesus toward his disciples when they expect the instant arrival of the Kingdom of God, as shown, for example, in the scene of the ascension (Ac 1:1-11). Jesus' disciples are upset that they still have not seen the realization of the Kingdom they understood was to come through him. As Jesus is about to depart they ask if this is the moment in which it is to come. Jesus' answer is, in effect, that it is all in the hands of God. They need to *wait;* the Kingdom will arrive when God decides the moment is right. In other words Jesus is saying, "Be patient because it is all in the hands of God."

Modern society educates people to expect instant results. A light is to go on as soon as the switch is flicked. Clocks are to be on time to the minute. Meetings, TV programs and church services are to start and end on schedule. People themselves are to be achievers, and these achievements are to be immediately perceptible. Even checking accounts are tallied daily for interest by computer.

NINES will find Jesus' teachings on the Kingdom of God very helpful as they seek to avoid the rat race of modern life. Jesus suggests in the parables of the Kingdom that God's pace in bringing about the Kingdom is like the pace of nature. The Kingdom will come gradually into people's lives. It is like a seed planted. It takes root slowly. Only after considerable time does it produce a harvest (Mt 13:4-9). This indicates that life with God takes patience. As shown in the evolution of the planet earth, God waited millions of years for the conditions of life to be ready for the appearance of human beings. Many more millennia passed before human beings developed the ability to record events and to put their stories into writing as history. Many more centuries passed before the human race began to have a sense of living a world history, with all nations as participants in one interdependent human family. God's designs take time to unfold in the world he has made. To join these designs with one's own life demands that a person be patient.

The Temptation to Indolence

NINES, of course, are adept at waiting; patience is no problem for them. Their pitfall, however, is *indolence*. To get in step with God's time does not mean people are to let God do everything while they simply wait for divine action to bring about the Kingdom. This problem of indolence developed among some Christians in the apostolic age because they were so sure the end of the world was imminent. At Thessalonica there were those who refused even to work to provide for themselves. St. Paul responded that he had never been idle when he was among them, nor did he abuse the hospitality of others. He gave as a rule that anyone who refused to work should not eat (2 Th 3:7-10). Similarly, the angels, after the ascension of Jesus, chided the disciples for standing there looking up into the sky (Ac 1:6-11). They were to follow Jesus' instructions by preparing themselves for the promised gift of the Spirit, after which they would go out into the world to use their gifts to change the world.

Using One's Gifts

NINES need to take seriously this promise of power from the Spirit. They are tempted to take life easy and succumb to their lack of energy. This comes from the failure to discover *within themselves* the resources they really have. They seek stimulation from without, waiting for someone else to get them involved in something, instead of living in a dynamic and creative way. Their indolence gives them a poor self-image and makes them feel empty. They indeed are gifted as persons but they will have a difficult time believing it as long as they don't make much happen!

Jesus promises his followers the experience of being empowered by God through the indwelling Spirit. This is the same gift of the Spirit that enlivened Jesus in all his activity. It serves to give persons confidence not only that God loves them, but that they are loved in the same way that Jesus is loved (Jn 17:26). They are to believe in God's faith in them. Having faith in each follower of Jesus, God entrusts to that person unique gifts along with the guidance of the Spirit in the development and use of those gifts. From this comes a call to *mission*. Each person is a special gift of God to the world. His or her life is designed by God to make a difference in how the world is. That influence on the world will come by the person getting in touch with her or his inner life and making a gift of that inner life to others.

With the gift of the Spirit there also comes an *inner peace* which follows from knowing God's personal love. The knowledge of this love leads the person to accept that he or she is truly lovable and frees the person to make a self-gift to others. Out of gratitude for knowing God's love, the person will want to help others also know they are loved. A way of doing this is simply to love them, for thereby Jesus' own love is given to them.

When love becomes mutual among Christians, Jesus promises a special presence of himself in their midst (Mt 18:20). By such *Christian community* the very life of the Blessed Trinity becomes present and experienced. Not to know such *communion of persons* is to miss experiencing God's own life (1 Jn 1:17-11). NINES need to listen to this teaching as a way out of indolence. By overcoming personal isolation through mutual love and dialogue with others, they are able to get in touch with the energy of God's own trinitarian life. In getting closer to others through shared faith and love, they find themselves growing in many ways. The horizons of their interests broaden and they have more energy in their lives.

To live in community means to search for ways to be at peace together. As St. Paul says, the gift of love is patient; it is always ready to excuse, to trust, to hope, to endure whatever comes (1 Cor 13:4-7). Love is the great bridge-builder, the great reconciler. Since the Spirit impels people from within to desire unity, NINES find through the Spirit new resources for bringing people together. They already have a natural ability to build community. The gift of the Spirit gets people to open up and share through dialogue. In this way NINES can discover they have leadership ability for building bonds between persons and helping them work through conflict and division. NINES need to take an initiative in encouraging people to let down their defenses by telling one another how each sees the situation and what each one needs. Words need to be found to label feelings as they are in a non-judgmental way, whether they be hurts or fears, excitement or boredom. If people listen to one another, they can remove misunderstanding and open a way for apologies and expressions of forgiveness. NINES can have a great aptitude for bringing to others the true value of community by helping them discover that *nothing is as important as union of persons.* Thereby people can share God's own trinitarian life.

PART TWO:
Understanding One's Compulsion

3. THE COMPULSIVE SELF
LOOKING AT THE WORLD

According to Oscar Ichazo, who brought the Sufi tradition of the Enneagram to the United States, ego consciousness is the result of "a split between the self and the world." As he explains,

> A contradiction develops between the inner feelings of the child and the outer social reality to which he must conform. Ego consciousness is the limited mode of awareness that develops as a result of the fall into society. Personality forms a defensive layer over the essence and so there is a split between the self and the world. The ego feels the world as alien and dangerous because it constantly fails to satisfy the deeper needs of the self.[19]

According to Ichazo, persons between the ages of four and six discover that the inner feelings they have of themselves are not "in synch" with the world around them. Society is in some way hostile to them. This is experienced as a *loss*. Initially they did not expect there would be any such contradiction between themselves and outer reality, but instead that they could achieve personal completeness, the realization of their deepest desires, through a union with exterior reality, which includes the whole cosmos and God within it. They decided to *compensate* for this loss of ideal unity between themselves and everything else by taking care of themselves in the matter of personal fulfillment. To do this there was a necessary limiting of awareness of what self-fulfillment is and of who they are. By deciding to create their own lives as the result of a break with the world of external reality they were saying they could fulfill themselves, and thereby refused to depend on *interdependence* with external reality for their own self-realization. Such an attitude of "self-salvation" actually constituted a sin of pride since others are not depended on for one's essential completeness as a person.

More will be said about this locked-in attitude about salvation in Chapters 5 and 6. Relating this phenomenon of ego consciousness to the nine personality types in the Enneagram is basic to the study of the compulsions in their cause. To do this an analysis is made of the various alternatives in forming an ego consciousness. This relates to the topic of *the self vis-a-vis the world*.

The Self vis-a-vis the World

According to Tad Dunne, S.J., the nine different kinds of ego consciousness in the Enneagram result from the *intersecting* of three distinct *self-concepts* and three distinct preferred *modes of behavior*.[20] The self-concepts are ways of looking at the self; the modes of behavior are ways of relating to the world.

The three distinct *self-concepts* are:

(a) "I am bigger than the world."

(b) "I must adjust to the world."

(c) "I am smaller than the world."

The three distinct preferred *modes of behavior* are:

(1) *against* the world (AGGRESSIVE behavior)
(2) *towards* the world (DEPENDENT behavior)
(3) *away from* the world (WITHDRAWING behavior)

From the *intersecting* of the three self-concepts and the three preferred modes of behavior, Dunne offers a schema of the enneagram types as shown in TABLE I.

TABLE I[21]

	(a) "I am bigger than the world."	(b) "I must adjust to the world."	(c) "I am smaller than the world."
(1) *AGGRESSIVE*	8	3	1
(2) *DEPENDENT*	2	6	7
(3) *WITHDRAWING*	5	9	4

(1) AGGRESSIVE TYPES: 8, 3, 1

The AGGRESSIVE TYPES, 8, 3, 1, have the preferred mode of behavior of *moving against people* as a defense strategy to protect the self and one's worth as a person. Each of the aggressive types has a different way of moving against others because each starts from a different self-concept:

(a) "I am bigger than the world" (#8). Since EIGHTS believe they are bigger than the world, they

move with an instinct of power against people. They are tough, often say no, tend to bully people, and see others as hypocritical. They *intimidate* others to throw them off balance. They deal with reality by beating it down. Their spontaneous reaction to any fear is not to back down or let anyone have an advantage over them, but to be assertive and aggressive. For EIGHTS, "to be" is "to be strong." They prove their worth or preserve their dignity by strength of personality.

(b) "I must adjust to the world" (#3). Because THREES think they must adjust to the world, their aggressive behavior is channeled into *achievement*. They think they prove their worth by successes. For them, "to be" is "to be successful."

(c) "I am smaller than the world" (#1). ONES express their aggressive behavior by being *critical of themselves* since they believe they need to work hard to do things well and thereby become worthwhile as persons. They also project this criticism onto others by expecting them to work hard at doing things right and to correct in themselves what is not right. The critical aggressivity of ONES puts them at odds with their surroundings, and even with themselves, because for them, "to be" is "to be perfect." Because they feel smaller than the world and move out against the world, they spend much conscious energy trying to get on top of the world. They experience life as always *working uphill.*

(2) DEPENDENT TYPES: 2, 6, 7.

The DEPENDENT TYPES, 2, 6, 7, have a preferred behavior of *moving toward people.* They defend their self-worth by becoming dependent on others through relationships. Because they start from a different self-concept, each type has a different way of being dependent:

(a) "I am bigger than the world" (#2). Since TWOS have a self-concept of being bigger than the world, they take an *initiative* in forming relationships. They do this by moving to make others feel cared for and cared about. Their *dependency approach in caring results from their reluctance to be served by others. They want to make others dependent on them* as the way to form relationships. For them, "to be" is "to be needed."

(b) "I must adjust to the world" (#6). Since SIXES have a self-concept that they must adjust to the world in order to be worthwhile, they place great importance on *conforming* to standards and laws already laid down. They see their self-worth dependent on *carrying out the responsibilities given them.* In their world, "to be" is "to be responsible."

(c) "I am smaller than the world" (#7). SEVENS grew up feeling smaller than the world. For them to feel alive their environment needs to be full of good times and good cheer. *Their self-worth depends on life being cheerful.* As a result they screen out whatever is painful or laborious from their perception. For them, "to be" is "to be cheerful."

(3) WITHDRAWING TYPES: 5, 9, 4.

The WITHDRAWING TYPES, 5, 9, 4, have a preferred behavior of *moving away from people* to enhance their sense of personal worth. They express this defense strategy of withdrawal in different ways in accordance with their different self-concepts:

(a) "I am bigger than the world" (#5). Since FIVES grew up with a self-concept of being bigger than the world, their withdrawal from people has as its purpose to become an intellectual *overseer* of everything. To keep on top of the world they think *they need to understand reality as it is* through their own study and reflection. For them, "to be" is "to be all-knowing."

(b) "I must adjust to the world" (#9). NINES withdraw from the world to adjust to it because it does not offer much to them in appreciation or love. This is both an act of *resignation* and a defense strategy to avoid conflict. They say there is nothing much happening anyway and expect little from themselves or others. *They seek contentment with whatever happens* since to them, "to be" is "to be content."

(c) "I am smaller than the world" (#4). Because FOURS have grown up thinking they are smaller than the world, they express their withdrawing behavior by feeling misunderstood and by *rehearsing* how to express themselves with greater originality and authenticity. They often feel the world is leaving them behind while *they await an experience of real life* with others. In their viewpoint, "to be" is "to be special."

A False Sense of Reality

According to Dunne, ego consciousness is characterized by *a false sense of reality,* i.e., what life is really about. Each of the three different self-concepts gives, as it were, a special "lens" through which to focus on fulfillment in life:

(a) Reality as the Inner Order: those who have an ego consciousness that says "I am bigger than the world" see real life as in the "inner order," i.e., as *centered on themselves.*

(b) Reality as Outer-inner Harmony: those saying "I must adjust to the world" see real life as a harmony or *integration between themselves and the outer world.*

(c) Reality as the Outer Order: those saying "I am smaller than the world" see real life, or fulfillment, as *centered outside themselves* in the environment.

In each case, the ego sees real life, or fulfillment, as attainable through its own efforts. These efforts differ according to three modes of behavior in seeking real life:

(1) *OFFENSIVE behavior:* the AGGRESSIVE TYPES, 8, 3, 1.
(2) *ACCEPTANCE behavior:* the DEPENDENT TYPES, 2, 6, 7.
(3) *DEFENSIVE behavior:* the WITHDRAWING TYPES, 5, 9, 4.

The above six intersecting categories are shown in the schema of TABLE II of the Enneagram types concerning *a false sense of reality.*

TABLE II[22]

	(a) *Reality as the Inner Order*	(b) *Reality as Outer-inner Harmony*	(c) *Reality as the Outer Order*
(1) *OFFENSIVE*	8 - control	3 - appearances	1 - shoulds
(2) *ACCEPTANCE*	2 - approval	6-apprehensions	7 - plans
(3) *DEFENSIVE*	5 - correctness	9 - harmony	4 - scripts

(1) OFFENSIVE TYPES: 8, 3, 1.

The OFFENSIVE TYPES, 8, 3, 1, seek to possess fulfillment by moving out *against others*. Their behavior differs according to the distinct lens through which they view real life:

(a) Reality as the Inner Order (#8). EIGHTS see life as real when they have *control* through their own inner strength. They say "To be fulfilled I must be strong over against others." They feel good about themselves only by retaining control. It is a matter of personal dignity for them to say, "Since I am strong, others do not step on me." To them *their own possession of control gives them a great sense of well-being,* which is derived from their self-concept that they are bigger than the world.

(b) Reality as Outer-inner Harmony (#3). THREES say, "To be fulfilled I must achieve success in other people's eyes." The good they seek aggressively consists actually in *appearances.* What they call success really is a *good image,* which is attained by the reaction of others. THREES do not see themselves fulfilled by achieving what is worthwhile irrespective of what others think; to be fulfilling the achievements must be successful in the sense of being known and favorably reacted to by others. Such success is a relationship of themselves with others caused by their accomplishments being esteemed by others, or, more precisely, that *they are esteemed because of their accomplishments.*

(c) Reality as the Outer Order (#1). ONES look to the outer order, the environment, for the fulfillment they seek. They see real life coming only if the situa-

tion is made better than it is. They move against their environment with the attitude that there are problems in life that need correction. They are great criticizers, both of themselves and others because for them reality is a matter of *shoulds*. They seek fulfillment in their lives by taking the offensive through criticism and hard work. *Only by correcting what is wrong and doing what is right externally can they see life being lived as it should be.*

(2) ACCEPTANCE TYPES, 2, 6, 7.

The ACCEPTANCE TYPES, 2, 6, 7, seek fulfillment by moving *towards others*. They see such fulfillment as something *accepted* or received. The way they move towards others for this fulfillment of real life varies according to the limited view, or "lens," each has concerning reality:

(a) Reality as the Inner Order (#2). TWOS say, "To be fulfilled as a person I must be needed." They don't feel they are good inside unless they have the *approval* or appreciation of another. They seek to please a preferred other to obtain that approval. Having obtained it, they then *accept themselves* as good. *Such self-acceptance is what they mainly seek in life.*

(b) Reality as Outer-inner Harmony (#6). SIXES say, "To be fulfilled I must satisfy the demands made on me." Satisfying these demands is seen by them *as assuring* a harmony between themselves and their environment. Since they experience the reality of life as constantly making demands on them, *they feel they are in contact with life only when they have apprehen-*

sions, i.e., fears about fulfilling what is expected of them. Such apprehensions keep them concerned about all their responsibilities and focused on what is fulfillment in life for them. To let go of these concerns would be to fail, in their view, to face up to life in what it asks of them.

(c) Reality as the Outer Order (#7). SEVENS see their fulfillment in making *plans* concerning what happens in their environment. They view life optimistically because they *accept* the plans they make as constituting what life is really about. To them, *life consists in making plans* for the future. These plans, as a consequence, often seem more real to them and more interesting, than anything that happens at the present moment.

(3) DEFENSIVE TYPES: 5, 9, 4

The DEFENSIVE TYPES, 5, 9, 4, seek fulfillment by *withdrawing* from others. They feel a need to *defend* themselves by a detachment from others. Only in this way do they see themselves as able to possess real life. What they seek to attain by this detachment or withdrawal differs in each according to the kind of "lens" used for viewing the reality of life:

(a) Reality as the Inner Order (#5). FIVES find fulfillment within themselves in their own correct judgment. It takes much time in their own private space to do the necessary study and reflection they think is needed to examine all points of view and gain an overall insight. To live this fullness of life they become possessive and stingy about their own time and seclusion. They are hesitant about explaining

what they have been thinking because the whole picture is very complex to them. It takes much study to see it all and before this is achieved they cannot be certain of having a correct judgment. *What they value above all is the correctness of their own judgment* based on objective knowledge. In their striving to attain this they are defensive regarding the intrusions of others into their private world where they believe they can find the fullness of life.

(b) Reality as Outer-inner Harmony (#9). NINES think that to have real life they must be at peace. The real life of peace they seek is a *harmony between themselves and their environment.* Because they experience the environment as conflictual and tension-producing, they back off from it. Even though such a life of peace is rather dull, they are satisfied with it because they think that is the best that can be expected in life.

(c) Reality as the Outer Order (#4). FOURS withdraw from others to rehearse *scripts,* i.e., to practice how they can become more authentic and original in the way they express themselves. They see their fulfillment as *the authentic expression of their unique feelings.* In their striving for fullness of life they keep trying to express symbolically the special feelings inside themselves.

A False Sense of Virtue and Vice

By limiting what life is to be through a false sense of reality, each Enneagram type has a different perspective in seeing what constitutes virtue and vice. Virtue concerns what moves a person towards a full

life and vice involves what contradicts such fulfillment. To have a false sense of reality, i.e., a myopic
view of what life is, results in *a false sense of virtue and
vice*. This prevents the person from recognizing the
change in attitude and repentance that is needed. Since
the person considers what actually is his or her
predominant fault to be a predominant virtue, no
remorse about the fault will be forthcoming. This false
sense of virtue and vice varies according to the "lens"
the person has for viewing the reality of life:

(a) Reality as the Inner Order: 8, 2, 5. Those Enneagram types with a self-concept that "I am bigger
than the world" limit what is good in life too much to
themselves. *What they mainly take pride in is how they
are* as persons.

#8. EIGHTS think they are good mainly because
they are strong persons over others. In their estima-
tion, to be real as a person is to ensure one's personal
dignity by being in control. This is why they often lack
any remorse of conscience when they intimidate
others. To them it is great virtue to be strong in relationship with others even though this involves being
arrogant. Similarly, they think it is a vice to be weak
before others or in any way to let themselves be taken
advantage of even though in actuality a gentle disposition is a virtue.

#2. TWOS think they are good mainly because
they are important to another for what they do for that
person. They think their helpfulness is a great virtue
despite the fact that by it they try to make another
need them. This manipulation of another occurs
because they deny they have any needs themselves.
They think their own denial of need is the virtue of be-

ing selfless when actually it involves the vice of manipulating another. Similarly, they think concern about their own needs would be the vice of selfishness when actually it would be a virtuous love of self.

#5. FIVES think they are good because they withdraw from others to understand how everything fits together. They consider it a virtue to be aloof and preoccupied with their own thoughts when actually such a living in their own world is a lack of generosity towards others. Since they feel wisdom means they must think things out all by themselves, they consider it a vice not to do all their thinking alone when actually to gather with others in reflective dialogue can often be more productive of wisdom, and thus can be virtuous. FIVES tend to think being a *loner* is a virtue when actually it is a vice.

(b) Reality as Outer-inner Harmony: 3, 6, 9. Those Enneagram types with a self-concept that "I must adjust to the world" limit what is good in life too much to accepting the world as it is and adjusting themselves to it. *What they mainly take pride in is their conforming to the world and its standards.* What their "world" is differs, of course, with each personality type.

#3. THREES think they are good because they move aggressively into the world through achievements which conform to what others hail as successes. For them, to be real one must achieve. They take pride in saying, "I am efficient." Their great blindness is thinking that success is a measure of one's true worth, of that which makes a person good. In reality, their notion of success is not a virtue but involves the vice of *vanity.* They may feel very guilty

about failing in something as though this calls for some kind of self-accusation. In actuality, acceptance of failure may fittingly be an expression of the *virtue of humility.*

#6. SIXES also concentrate on fitting themselves into the world in order to consider themselves as good persons. They live in apprehension and fear about the demands life makes on them in the form of responsibilities. In order to be persons of worth it is important to them to fulfill all external duties through faithful obedience to laws and regulations given by authority. They make a fetish of obedience to law as though all virtues were simply matters of obeying laws,and all vices were the breaking of laws. By restricting virtue exclusively to outward obedience, they have a false sense of all virtue. In actuality, *true virtue is a committed response to values considered as absolutes,* such as the values of love and mercy. SIXES make virtues a commitment to obeying laws whereas actually all laws are judged by the absolute values to which virtues are committed. SIXES have a propensity to fall into the vice of self-righteousness, which is the classic way of mistaking vice for virtue by *being proud that one never commits any real sin.*

#9. NINES seek to get in contact with what is good by being settled and peaceful through a *detachment* from the world outside themselves. They adjust to the world by avoiding whatever will disrupt their peace. They consider this detachment to be a virtue; they are proud of being so easy-going. In actuality, they are exercising the *vice of sloth.* Similarly, they think that trying to correct the injustices of the whole world is a vice of presumption and results in the vice of

restlessness. They typically make a virtue of routine life and fail to see themselves and others called to a dedication for the welfare of the entire human community in this world even though such a dedication is a passionate expression of the virtue of justice.

(c) Reality as the Outer Order: 1, 7, 4. Those Enneagram types who see themselves as smaller than the world will place their energy into what they see as good outside themselves. In doing so, *they limit what is good too much to the environment,* and may make themselves slaves to achieving change in external reality. They do not sufficiently accept the value of their own inner good nor the importance of getting along with others despite the imperfections of external reality. They take pride in doing what will bring about changes in the environment by putting themselves into the flow of reality outside themselves.

#1. ONES are blind to their own *resentment,* which is really the capital sin called *anger.* Instead of seeing it as the vice it is, they think their own critical standards are expression of great virtue. They do not appreciate sufficiently the virtue of *self-acceptance;* instead they think that the greatest vice is to stop trying to be better or do better.

#7. SEVENS see sadness and pessimism as great vices when actually such attitudes can be a truthful reaction to reality as actually experienced by a person. They mistake constant cheerfulness as a great virtue when at least sometimes a more sober attitude would be much more appropriate. They tend to make a god of enjoying pleasures to the detriment of the virtue of temperance or moderation. They think seriousness in people is a vice when actually it may be an expression

of authenticity, i.e., truthfulness about how a person really is or how life is actually being faced.

#4. FOURS make a god of their sensitivity and think it a great vice to be uncouth. They make a virtue of being unique in the sense of being better than others, or more important when actually that attitude is the vice of *vainglory.* They think being ordinary is a vice when actually it may be the great virtue of *simplicity.*

The Experience of Time

Another way in which the compulsive self looks at the world is through one's relationship with *time.* Time involves change: objectively it is a *measure of change in external reality.* Inside each person there is an internal clock used to measure transitions in that person's experience.

Each Enneagram type will have its own kind of time consciousness because each type perceives reality differently, as illustrated in FIGURE 2.

#1. ONES feel *dominated* by time. They experience it as a force that pulls or drags them against their own will. Because they sense there is not enough time to get things right, they feel resentful about time. Often it seems to them that their feet are caught in a treadmill of time and they cry out, "Wait a minute," as they try to halt the time drain. They want to say, "Let's slow this down so we can get it right; let's go over this again to make sure we've got it right." They keep wanting to go back over things, drawing the other into their own time frame, until they feel the

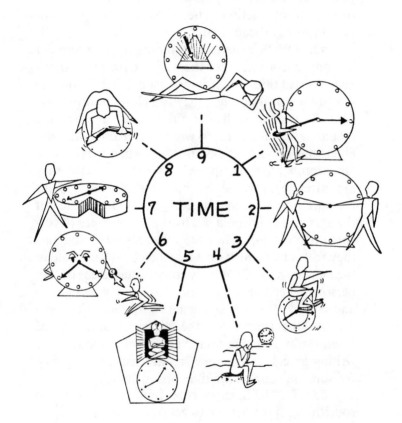

FIGURE 2

point they are insisting on has really been finished to their own satisfaction. Then they want to go to the next most significant item.

#2. TWOS experience time as opportunity for personal encounters. For them a good time is *interpersonal;* a bad time is non-interpersonal. To them there is a full use of time when they feel closer to other persons. They tend to live in the time of another and manipulate that person to win that person's time and enter into it. Time drags for them when they cannot enter into a relationship well. As a consequence, they are often aggravated by business meetings. They measure time at such a meeting not by how much of the agenda was covered but by their experience of personal relationship. They are very sensitive to anyone they feel is being hurt or threatened by what is said at the meeting and will quickly come to the rescue of that person. When matters get impersonal they may get up and serve coffee or open a window for more air. Some prepare themselves for the expected boredom of meetings by bringing their knitting or stationery for writing letters so that they can at least do something for someone during the time of the meeting.

#3. THREES experience time as a means to something. It is a vehicle to get somewhere, an instrument for accomplishment, a tool for productivity. Time is something to be *used*. It measures goals and objectives. Every minute of it must be used, otherwise it represents a lost opportunity. THREES experience time as limited; it is not expandable. After the deadline is too late. Consequently they adjust their goals to how much time is available. Because they are achievers, they tend to take on too much for the time available,

and as a result they usually run a little late, but they are fully aware of this and make accommodations along the way. Though they want to start on time and end on time that need is secondary to getting the job done. For them when something has been accomplished time has been well spent. They are often puzzled when others seem to need so much time just "for themselves," especially when this means things are not done on time.

#4. In FOURS, the sense of time is very subjective and is measured by *emotional intensity.* When they are emotionally involved in something, they find that time flies; otherwise it drags. They tend to be late because they lose track of clock time though they will be early for an appointment when they anticipate it as an experience of deep involvement. Nostalgia and melancholy often hinder their insertion into the present moment. They experience the past as unfinished, filled with lost opportunities as well as emotional experiences they need fathom more deeply. In narrating the past they typically do not list events chronologically but begin with whatever was more emotionally engaging or beautiful.

#5. FIVES typically *watch* time go by as though they were in the clock looking out at a series of significant moments or experiences. As they watch things happen, they reflect on everything so as to reconstruct it in a meaningful way. In narrating the past, they tell about each individual experience and its significance in chronological order. To them there is always something interesting happening, and if it isn't occurring outside themselves, then it can happen inside. They don't like any one thing to drag on because there

are so many other things to comprehend and observe; when this affair is over, they want immediately to move on to the next so they can know it. They are able to get much done in a given amount of time, but they say that there was not enough time because they want to do something original and thorough. Since time is needed to be thorough they are miserly with it. They resent the fact that they don't have time to look at everything and understand it.

#6. In SIXES, time is boss. The clock is an *authority* to be reckoned with. They have to submit to it even though this causes conflict within them. Time is a series of threats. The real issue is danger. Because they see things needing to be done with dispatch, they get work done incredibly fast. They fear they will make mistakes if they dally. Deadlines are very important; they try very hard to keep them, otherwise they will be in trouble. Time judges their faithfulness to duty. The issue is to respond to the demands constantly made on them. Typically they arrive on time and leave on time. Time is not their personal possession. Rather, it is a measure of responsibility to others.

#7. For SEVENS, time is like a huge pie that can be sliced into an infinite number of pieces; only a slice has already been taken and there are so many more! To them time is always *expandable.* As long as they are having fun there is always enough time, and they keep adding one thing after another. As a consequence, they have trouble being on time. Often their enjoyment is future oriented; they already experience the future before it comes because of the way they plan and anticipate things. Because the planning is so important and exciting to them, they are often content

with having had the idea rather than buckling down to achieving it. They procrastinate because getting down to the details is not fun, and so they tend to put them out of their minds.

#8. EIGHTS don't let time control them; they *control* it. They are determined to make the clock go at their own pace. Not only are they punctual, but they often arrive ahead of time so that the clock need not be attended to. They experience time as stretching out flatly with few features of interest. They decide what is significant and make this a milestone by which to measure time. Once they get involved in what is significant to them, time is no issue and is not measured. They find it difficult to know when they are going to arrive at their goal, so they are concerned to keep moving. This gives them a quiet impatience and puts a momentum into their activities so that they keep going with the same speed and inexorable force.

#9. NINES have a *metronomic* sense of time. Each moment has the same duration and each event the same importance. They sense that there is too much to do within the time and so they keep at it. The important thing is to stay on schedule and to keep the emotional content low. They need schedules and are easily upset by any change in their schedule. They have no way of squeezing any new thing into their schedule and will have to add it on after they have done everything else. To them being on time or not being on time isn't terribly important as long as they stay with it. Their response to overload is just to keep at it and not be upset.

Totems of the Compulsive Types

In the way they relate to the world the compulsive personality types of the Enneagram can be seen as resembling specific animals. These amusing, sometimes insightful, *totems* of their behavior are shown in FIGURE 3. Such totems can be aptly replaced by another set when the types become healed, or "redeemed," as will be shown in Chapter 6.

#1. The compulsive ONE is like a *terrier*. Terriers are little dogs that can inflict terror. They bite first and then bark. They are never sure the other is an adversary but they bite first just in case. They are never at rest but are always worrying about whatever is going on around them. They do tend to overestimate themselves in setting things right. Because ONES impose their own standards of perfection on others they tend to make it their business "to snap at heels" by pointing out what isn't being done right. When hurt by another they will talk about the hurt to anyone except the person involved, for they feel it is not good behavior to confront and they expect the other to know what is required and to do it.

#2. The compulsive TWO is like a *cat*. Cats come up and rub against a person until they are satisfied and then stroll away. They may turn on the person, however, if he or she gets too close. Cats are sneaky and creep up from behind a corner. They love to stare at a person but don't like to be stared at. Like cats, TWOS are affectionate but carry an air of independence in not letting another serve them.

#3. The compulsive THREE is like a *peacock*. Peacocks are barnyard showoffs and flash their rear

FIGURE 3

feathers at everyone. They pick up little bits and pieces and can make use of anything. Like peacocks, THREES demand attention by vain strutting; their focus is on whatever will get others to like them.

#4. The compulsive FOUR is like a *basset hound*. In basset hounds the ears and eyes compete for the lowest droop. Water flows from the sides of their faces. A person can pick up the skin and leave the dog behind. They wag their tails like a mop on a wet floor. They are beggars for scraps from the table and accept garbage for the real thing. Like basset hounds, FOURS express sadness as a way to be in connection with others. As another person tries to get hold of FOURS, they sit in their sadness because they feel not really understood.

#5. The compulsive FIVE is like a *fox*. Foxes slink around and hole up in dark logs. Their main source of livelihood is carrion. They become infested by what they bite and are a prey to diseases found in dark holes. Despite their fairly large size, they choose only small prey. Like foxes, FIVES have an intense gaze; they slink around on the edge of things and tackle only small things that won't get them into too much of life. They know what is happening around them because they have watched it.

#6. The compulsive SIX is like a *rabbit*. Rabbits are alert but are always twitching. When scared they bolt, running this way and that with such hysteria that they often run into their pursuer. Though they are pugnacious fighters, they fight alone and so often end up in a predator's stomach. They are noted for reproducing more and more of the same. Like rabbits, SIXES often feel extremely vulnerable and live with

much apprehensiveness and indecision.

#7. The compulsive SEVEN is like a *monkey.* Monkeys are noisy and also very inquisitive. They make strange noises and like to get into fights. They live literally in the air, leaping from branch to branch. Like monkeys, compulsive SEVENS look all around because they want to be ready for life. They talk much, telling gossipy stories. They do seem to be up in the air because they have so many things going on in their life and can always juggle more.

#8. The compulsive EIGHT is like a *rhinoceros.* Despite their fearsome size rhinos are vegetarians. They are nearsighted and thick-skinned. Whatever they don't recognize they gore or topple. Like rhinos, EIGHTS charge first and ask questions later. They stomp on another first to make sure they won't get hurt. EIGHTS will say, "Don't pull that crying stunt on me."

#9. The compulsive NINE is like an *elephant.* Elephants are ponderous. They are so big they even step on their own young, seemingly unaware of their own massiveness and weight. They trample their own food and denude their surroundings before moving again. Out of curiosity they take things in their trunks and sometimes suffocate themselves. Like elephants compulsive NINES are ponderous because they think they have to be at the center of being. They sit down and seem unaware of their own weight in the situation. They tend to be unwilling to move on to a new place. They want to be taken along by others, rather than be responsible for moving. Like elephants they are all ears, but their ears cover up their ability to hear.

4. THE UNBALANCED SELF

In each Enneagram type *a limited good* has been turned into *the absolute good* of the personality. Whatever the self sees as absolute good will be loved *passionately* from the deepest sources of responsive energy in a person. It is this passionate love that creates the defensive strategy, called the compulsion, which serves to protect, attain and maintain the goal of fulfillment. That goal in life was chosen as a result of experiencing the world as being alienating, i.e., society seemed to contradict the deepest feelings and desires of the self. In view of this felt alienation, a choice was made of how to save oneself, to find fulfillment for the self by choosing a certain way to be a person. This constituted a limitation of the human essence, a narrowing down of the way to express the giftedness of being a human person.[23] Had that limitation or narrowing-down of the essence not taken place, there would have arisen no compulsion in the personality, as has been exemplified in the personality of Jesus. He was the first truly human being. By allowing himself to express all the aspects of human essence in his personality he avoided the *imbalance* of humanness caused by seeking to defend some one way of being human. It also meant that Jesus did not seek to save himself against an alien world through the defensive strategy called a compulsion.

Although passionate love is the fundamental energy in a human being because it pursues personal fulfillment, when the goal of fulfillment is not the fullness of human essence but rather some limitation of it, the result is that passionate love becomes *distorted* by what are called *passions*. Such passions are not a corruption of human nature; they are simply a distortion in the person's response to absolute good. The distortion is caused not by some poison within, but by a mistake made in what constitutes the absolute good of fulfillment for the person. It is a mistake caused by a false sense of reality.

The Passions

The Enneagram showing the dominant *passion* characterizing each personality type is shown in FIGURE 4. The distortion in passionate love is further explicated in FIGURES 5, 6 and 7, according to the three mistakes in viewing reality as a person's self-fulfillment.

(a) Reality as the Inner Order: 8, 2, 5. Here each type is characterized by a passion centering on oneself.

#8. — arrogance. EIGHTS overdo the assertion of themselves by the passion of *arrogance,* i.e., by *telling the truth to another without love.* They are dedicated to truth and justice but the way they express this to others has the defensive strategy of protecting themselves by overpowering the other. They see life as a power struggle and passionately are dedicated to being strong and avoiding all weakness in themselves. Their dedication to their own fulfillment of being strong persons does not take into account the human need to find fulfillment through union with others. To EIGHTS it is an end in itself to "have it out" with another rather than to see such exchange of opinion as a way to reconciliation and union. They take pride in

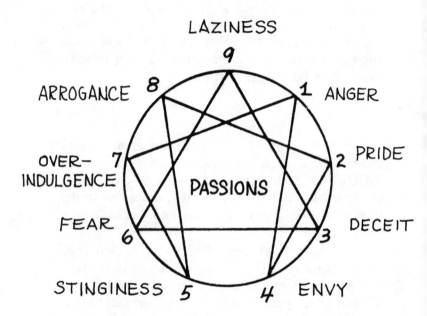

FIGURE 4

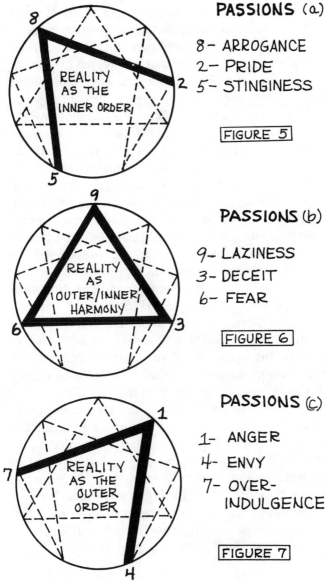

PASSIONS (a)

8- ARROGANCE
2- PRIDE
5- STINGINESS

FIGURE 5

PASSIONS (b)

9- LAZINESS
3- DECEIT
6- FEAR

FIGURE 6

PASSIONS (c)

1- ANGER
4- ENVY
7- OVER-
   INDULGENCE

FIGURE 7

holding their own rather than being humble enough to grow in intimate union with others. Because of an initial experience in life of alienation, perhaps by being overpowered by a dominant parent, they decided that to protect themselves they must always put up a strong front and never give in. Only in that way did they think they could attain what they chose to be their absolute good, namely, the maintenance of personal strength in the face of an alien world. Although they probably would agree that might does not make right, their passionate love seeks that which keeps them in control, and for the sake of being in control the intimidation of another through arrogance is a worthwhile endeavor. Because such experiences of fulfillment never give the heart the feeling of truly having attained possession of an unlimited, absolute good, the passion of the EIGHT sometimes *craves* the experience of personal power by going around looking for a fight. No matter how many experiences EIGHTS have of personal strength vis-a-vis another, more are craved because strength before others was chosen as an unlimited good of the personality. No one experience of personal power, nor any series of such experiences, will ever completely fill the quest of the unlimited good of personal fulfillment. Moreover, any threatening of the EIGHT'S sense of personal dignity by someone else taking over control, or assuming to give orders to the EIGHT, is resisted spontaneously by the passion of arrogance. This arrogance attempts to make the other person back off. EIGHTS like to give orders but find it very repugnant to take orders, because that contradicts their distorted passion for self-fulfillment.

    #2. — pride. TWOS also center their passionate

love on themselves. It is expressed as the passion of *pride* which means *not to need another*. There is a deep contradiction in this, for the TWO actually does need approval by those he or she serves. The stance of TWOS, however, is to deny personal need to attain what they see as their own fulfillment. They express spontaneously a denial of any need whatever when another suggests serving them in some way. Actually they try to keep control by having others need them. This serves to give TWOS a sense of self-fulfillment. This fulfillment is pride in themselves for being helping persons and not seeking anything in return. Because such a sense of oneself is made an absolute good, TWOS are uncomfortable with themselves when they are not actively *doing something* for another. The passionate power of this pride of TWOS is displayed when another fails to respond with approval or appreciation to their service. That hurts the TWOS' pride. Not to be needed means they are rejected as worthwhile persons. This passion of pride will react in a surprisingly acrid belittling of that person or in other acts of revenge. All along, the TWO lacked the *humility* to accept fulfillment in mutual and reciprocal service, especially through personal communion with others; instead, fulfillment was seen by TWOS as centered on themselves through approval of their helpfulness by another.

#5. — *stinginess*. The way FIVES center their passionate love on themselves is through the passion of *stinginess*. Their lack of generosity stems from making into an unlimited, absolute good the attainment of knowledge stored within themselves. They do not see their fulfillment through union with another, and this is evidenced by the reaction of their heart when a friend intrudes into their private space or interrupts the time they have set aside for their study projects. Since their fulfillment is never completely attained and they remain with a feeling of emptiness or ignorance, they have a craving to possess whatever time and solitude they can garner. Clinging to that solitude becomes the object of passionate love because they want to attain by it some sense of personal fulfillment. Without the solitude they feel they are losing their lives.

Because there is always more to know and one insight leads to more questions and reasons to do research, a sense of complete fulfillment eludes them. The only way they can satisfy the craving is by being *stingy* with their time. Thus they avoid any commitments that entangle them with others or prevent them from continuing their private projects for obtaining wisdom.

(b) Reality as Outer-inner Harmony: 3, 6, 9. Those types which see their fulfillment centering on a harmony with the world as it is will have their passionate love distorted through some kind of conforming to society as it is.

#3—deceit. THREES see their fulfillment in *appearances.* They want a good image before others, and this is attained by achievements which are recognized as successful. Because what others think is deemed by THREES as an unlimited, absolute good, they tend to hide from others whatever would hinder the success they desire. As a result, passionate love will seek to deceive. Such deceit begins when THREES put their own feelings in a sack for the sake of presenting a good

front before others. Even what is true becomes secondary to the absolute value they place on efficiency and accomplishments. The innate deceitfulness of THREES becomes more apparent in shady business deals, in the tactics used in business competition and in cheating on taxes as a way to ensure greater financial success. Because no one success ever fills the heart with an unlimited good, THREES crave success after success. This is usually seen as achieved through competition with others even through tactics of deceit.

#6—fear. The passionate love of SIXES seeks to conform to the outer reality of the world by responding to all its demands. Reality is experienced by SIXES in the form of apprehensiveness so they tend to be governed by the passion of *fear.* To acquit themselves of all that is demanded of them means they are often driven by apprehension. They are afraid they will be seen as not fulfilling their duties, especially when they are faced with uncertainty about what is right or wrong. Sometimes these fears are translated into *anxiety,* i.e., the fear of the unknown, especially the unknown future. SIXES fear change because what is known in the past is often seen by them as a safe guide to what is right or wrong. Because "custom is the best interpreter of law," that which overturns the customary ways of doing things is a great threat to the security of SIXES. They find fulfillment in conforming to the demands of authority. The passion of fear in SIXES is often evidenced in their over-seriousness concerning any kind of deviance from laws or traditional customs and the absoluteness and stubborness with which they often assert their authority in decisions and orders. Such "stonewalling" stems from the depths of a passionate love for conformity.

#9—laziness. NINES seek to conform to the world by withdrawing to take things easy. Harmony is made a god, an absolute good for them. They feel most at peace with themselves and others when they are doing little or nothing. Their response to excitement or conflict is to back away and dampen its importance. Instead of seeking fulfillment through involvement with others, they think their fulfillment is in being content to be by themselves, watching TV, collecting knickknacks or just taking it easy. Their innate inclination to inactivity is an effect of passionate love seeking contentment by doing nothing and thus expressing the passion of *laziness.*

(c) Reality as the Outer Order: 1, 7, 4. When fulfillment is seen to be centered in the environment, passionate love focuses on what is outside the person.

#1—anger. ONES do not readily admit that the main distortion of their response to reality is the passion of *anger.* They deny any anger in their hearts, yet their very approach to self-fulfillment channels passionate love into angry feelings. The good of perfection they seek is in terms of *doing things perfectly.* They continually see things not in right order, not done neatly or correctly. The result is a reaction of anger on their part. That anger is often expressed in being critical, and is frequently turned in on themselves because they have a self-concept of being smaller than the world. They see fulfillment as consisting in things being perfect; but the world is not perfect and they resent this. Such anger says to others that doing things correctly is more important to ONES than having people relate harmoniously with one another. The anger of ONES results from a mistake

that perfection is more important in life than accepting whatever gifts there are in life, imperfect as they yet may be. When the absolute good is made exterior perfection, the craving for an unlimited good is continually thwarted by any messiness or immaturity. The result is that passionate love gives stress to relatively unimportant details with an insistence on correcting things that disrupt the ability of ONES to live with others in harmony. Others feel imposed upon by all the fussiness and meticulousness of ONES; they do not feel at home with what anger does to the ONE's personality.

#7—*over-indulgence.* In their avoidance of pain in life, SEVENS seek all forms of pleasure as fulfillment. This distorts their passionate love into the passion of *over-indulgence* which often takes the form of gluttony or intemperance. Over-indulgence is caused by making pleasure an absolute good. Because every pleasure is, in fact, only a limited good, the quest to extract from it an unlimited good causes excess in the use of pleasure. One pleasure must then be followed continually by another if there is to be any sense of it being unlimited. This craving for unlimited pleasure is what causes SEVENS to do so much planning because the possibility of its attainment has to be projected into the ever-expandable future.

#4—*envy.* FOURS have a self-concept of being smaller than the world. They are trying to become more authentic persons as expressed through their *style.* They see as their fulfillment an authentic symbolic expression of themselves. Because their poor self-concept makes them compare themselves with others, they tend to be envious or jealous of anyone who stands out in the eyes of others. The style of the other is seen as competing with their own specialness. This passion of *envy* often surprises others because it seems so contradictory to the FOUR'S refinement. It does coincide, however, with the snobbishness so typical of FOURS, whereby they belittle another as having less refinement than they do. Anyone who stands out as a very special person because he or she has a striking personality causes feelings of envy in the FOUR. Instead of seeing the admiration of another's gifts as a way to interpersonal communion, FOURS see such giftedness as a threat to their own self-fulfillment, which is equated with the expression of themselves in dress, decor of their living quarters and their whole style of living and being.

Moving with the Arrows of Compulsion

A further upsetting of balance in the self occurs in the Enneagram types by what is called "moving with the arrows." The Enneagram is characterized not only by nine points around a circle but also by intersecting inner lines marked with *arrows*. The arrows indicate a relationship between the various types according to a movement toward greater compulsion, as shown in FIGURE 8. Tad Dunne sees these arrows of increased compulsion as following a general pattern based on whether the perfect *mode of behavior* of the ego is (1) AGGRESSIVE, (2) DEPENDENT, or (3) WITH-DRAWING. This pattern of increased compulsion is shown in FIGURE 9.

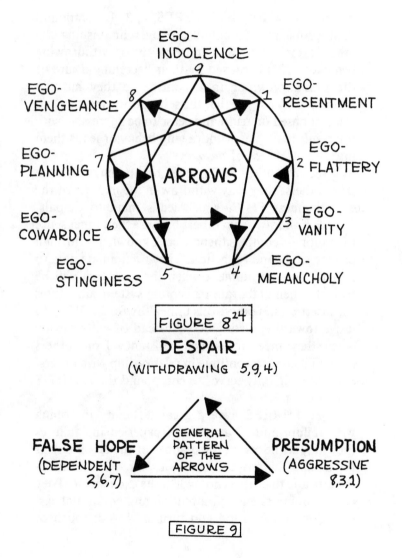

FIGURE 8[24]

DESPAIR
(WITHDRAWING 5,9,4)

FALSE HOPE
(DEPENDENT 2,6,7)

GENERAL PATTERN OF THE ARROWS

PRESUMPTION
(AGGRESSIVE 8,3,1)

FIGURE 9

(1) AGGRESSIVE TYPES: 8, 3, 1.

The AGGRESSIVE TYPES, 8, 3, 1, compound their problems of compulsion by relinquishing aggressive behavior and moving into withdrawing behavior. This is caused by their becoming aware of the *presumption* or false confidence they have in themselves. They see that the self-confidence they had was not based on truth and cease to be aggressive with the result that their withdrawing behavior leads them into the blackness of *despair*.

#8. When EIGHTS meet too much resistance from others, they may withdraw in the manner of the ego-stinginess FIVE, which leads them to despair. FIVES withdraw from others because their inner sense of emptiness compels them to seek knowledge through private study and reflection. They accumulate data to prepare for the moment when their wisdom will be sought. Their elaborate perceptual system substitutes for insertion in reality. It is unhealthy for EIGHTS to move toward ego-stinginess. Instead of withdrawing when they meet too much resistance from others EIGHTS need to continue in relationship with others. Withdrawing only serves to compound the EIGHT'S compulsion.

#3. THREES have a great difficulty in coping with failure and as a result of experiencing failures they may withdraw in the manner of the ego-indolent NINE and thereby end up in *despair*. NINES adopt the attitude that life is not worth the excitement. They exhibit minimal energy, attention and emotional caring. Conflict, decision and turmoil do not touch or

move them. Everything is brought down to the same level. They appear at home with being but are really anesthetized to life. The ego-indolent NINE is no model for THREES when failure causes them to doubt themselves. For THREES to become inactive like the ego-indolent NINE only compounds their compulsion. If they seek not only to avoid failure but also *to avoid conflict* by giving up their natural efficiency and organization, the result will be the blackness of despair. It is unhealthy for THREES to become inactive; they need regular activity which gives them reason for hoping and living.

#1. ONES may experience a mountain of work and feel unable to do any of it. They may react by completely giving up all their attempts to become perfect and thus follow the arrow of compulsion by taking on the withdrawal behavior of the ego-melancholy FOUR. FOURS make ordinary suffering tragic and dramatic. Their experience becomes so special that it becomes unreal. They usually feel that other people cannot understand them. They make themselves too special to fit in and thereby feel alone and misunderstood. ONES are not typically depressed; generally they find much fun in life. When they feel they cannot attain the perfection they think is necessary to them, they may end up not trying at all and move to *despair* by also taking on the compulsion of the ego-melancholy FOUR.

(2) DEPENDENT TYPES: 2, 6, 7.

The DEPENDENT TYPES, 2, 6, 7, see their fulfillment in terms of adapting to the world as it is.

When they sense that they are living a false hope and will not be able to attain the object of their fulfillment, their insecurity may lead them to move with the arrow toward the mode of behavior characteristic of the AG-GRESSIVE TYPES. This compounds their problem by moving them from false hope to *presumption,* i.e., an unsubstantiated confidence in themselves.

#2. TWOS may move with the arrow toward the ego-vengeance of the EIGHT when someone significant to them does not reciprocate with appreciation and approval of their service. They considered the other to be a super-special friend and the lack of reciprocation makes them feel crushed. As a result they take on the aggressiveness typical of the ego-vengeance EIGHT. EIGHTS experience themselves in a contest with unfriendly reality. They own their power but disown their gentleness. They are quick to negate and slow to affirm. Bearing a sledgehammer, EIGHTS instinctively attack the facade they assume separates them from reality. TWOS compound their problems when they seek revenge in the way characteristic of the EIGHT. TWOS will take such revenge by belittling their former super-special friend through backbiting. They find it difficult to confront people openly, but in their feelings of revenge they are saying, "I strike you from the land of the living."

#6. When SIXES experience great insecurity they may move with the arrow toward the hyper-activity and aggressivity characteristic of the ego-vanity THREE. THREES are very image-conscious. They so become their role that they lose themselves. Proving self-worth and seeking identity make them compulsive in doing and achieving. Efficiency becomes a god. By

moving toward the ego-vanity THREE, SIXES may take on some idealized role and compound their indecision with frantic activity and a feigned decisiveness. This is an attempt to cover up uncertainty by aggressive behavior. By that SIXES move from false hope to *presumption,* i.e., an unsubstantiated self-confidence.

#7. When SEVENS begin to realize their plans are not working out, they may move from that awareness of false hope to the presumption characteristic of the ego-resentment ONE and thereby move from an adapting mode of behavior to aggressive behavior typical of the ONE. ONES are obsessed with an unreal perfection. This obsession impels them to set themselves, others and the world right. Inability to create this perfection produces an acidic inner anger which leaches out in expressions of resentment.

When SEVENS move toward the compulsion of the ONE, they give up their usual optimism and begin to ask, "Why is this *always* happening?" They become prone to moodiness and all of a sudden their friends have become enemies. By reacting aggressively with resentment to an awareness that they had a false hope in their plans, they compound their problem by moving into the *presumption* characteristic of ONES.

(3) WITHDRAWING TYPES: 5, 9, 4.

The WITHDRAWING TYPES, 5, 9, 4, tend to compound their compulsiveness by moving with the arrow toward the mode of behavior of DEPENDENT TYPES. In so doing, they react to the despair they feel by clinging to some *false hope.*

#5. Ordinarily FIVES have their feet on the ground; they are realists. Dislike for their environment, however, could cause them to insulate themselves by letting their aloofness take them out of reality in the manner of ego-planning SEVENS. SEVENS avoid and deny whatever is painful. They white-wash the unpleasant. They sublimate pain, work and serious matters into stories, fantasies and plans. By moving into the compulsive dependent behavior typical of the SEVEN, FIVES begin to live in a fantasy world. It is unhealthy for FIVES not to be thinking about putting real things into action. When they live in pipe dreams they become all the more withdrawn and no longer reflect on what is really significant. It is a false hope for fulfillment. They have moved from despair caused by dislike for the world to the false hope of finding real life in what actually is a world of their own fantasy.

#9. When NINES begin to become aware of their problem of indolence they may lose all hope in themselves, and experience black despair. As a reaction to this they may try to flee from despair by moving with the arrow to the compulsion of the ego-cowardice SIX. SIXES tend to be extremely *unsure* of themselves. They lack the capacity and confidence to act effectively on their own. They combat self-doubt and indecision by placing their faith in authority outside themselves. By moving with the arrow toward the ego-cowardice SIX, NINES begin to worry about little things and take on a sense of over-responsibility. They become indecisive and dutiful in the manner of the SIX'S compulsion. They add *scruples* to their indolence. This is very unhealthy for them. They are say-

ing, "I'm not okay, I never was okay and I never will be okay."

#4. When FOURS come to a state of despair, they may react by clinging to another int he manner of the ego-flattery TWO. By moving with the arrow they assume the dependent behavior characteristic of the TWO and re-build their lives on a false hope which will be very destructive both to them and to the person they draw into their lives. TWOS are dependent upon the expressed appreciation, attention and approval of other people; otherwise they do not feel good about themselves. They have little sense of identity apart from their ability to help another. They project, repress and deny their own needs. FOURS do not normally cling to another; they do not try to tie another to them. When they do cling to another it is to save themselves from despair. This may occur when they begin to realize they are getting farther and farther from reality in their brooding over the tragedy of their past lives. Such desperate clinging to another has often been romanticized in literature by stories of lovers who are outcasts in society and cling to one another as their passionate love leads them to a death together.

The Personality Types
according to Their Preferred Center

The imbalance in the self caused by the compulsion of the Enneagram is especially portrayed by the theory of the "three centers." According to this theory, the self has three centers for functioning with the use of conscious and dynamic energy. These centers are designated as (A) the gut center, (B) the heart center and (C) the head center.

(A) The *gut center* functions with instincts and habits. It is also called the instinctive center, the moving center or the vital center. It is concerned with *being*. It moves spontaneously, often in reaction to an external stimulus. To live on the instinctive level is especially an experience of living in one's body and letting the body react to a present situation.

(B) The *heart center* functions on the level of feelings. It is also called the emotional or feeling center. It is mainly concerned about relationships with other persons. To live on a feeling level is experienced as the way of achieving personal encounter with others.

(C) The *head center* functions on the level of thinking and reflecting. It is also called the intellectual or thinking center, or the doing center. To think means to step back from reality as perceived and to reconstruct it according to some pattern or meaning. Such thinking is related to doing because action is the result of a conscious decision. To live on a thinking level is to experience being reflective within oneself and to act with considerable deliberation.

It is characteristic of each center that it is able to exercise not only its own proper function, but also can substitute for one or both of the other centers. One can use a given center not only for its own functioning but also to do the work of the other centers. This gives each center a certain autonomy. The gut center can use its instinctive function also for feeling and thinking; the heart center can use its feeling function also for thinking and instinctive movements; the head center can use its thinking function also for instinctive movements and for feeling. To substitute thus for another center can at times be helpful and even necessary. This can be readily seen where the thinking center substitutes for the instinctive function, when thinking is needed for acquiring a habit. While learning to type, for example, the head center consciously directs the fingers to the proper keys. The experienced typist, however, uses the instinctive center for typing; to use the head center in such a case would result in making mistakes. Pyotr Ouspensky, in his book *In Search of the Miraculous,* which deals extensively with the diverse centers, gives the example of a new recruit and an old soldier at a rifle drill. The recruit has not yet acquired the habits needed for the drill, so he performs the drill with his head center, thinking out each movement. The old soldier, on the other hand, performs the drill from instinct, and thus the old soldier does it better.[25]

In the Enneagram personality types *the ego consciousness has chosen some one of three centers as the way to be a person* to the detriment of the functioning of the other two centers. This results in an *imbalance* in functioning as a human being. Ideally the three centers are used interdependently with each center used for its own functioning in any given situation. This amounts to accepting one's whole human essence; no one center predominates by regularly substituting its functioning for that of one or both of the other centers. To choose some one center as the way to be a person disrupts the inner harmony of energy, narrows down the experience of being a person and creates an imbalance or awkwardness in the self. Instead of dwelling in each of the centers according to what is appropriate in the circumstances and using their mutual functioning like a team, the ego consciousness causes persons to identify with some one center and to make its functioning predominate as the way for them to experience life and to be themselves.

FIGURE 10 shows the Enneagram divided according to the three centers indicating the preferred functioning of each of the nine types. The GUT PERSONS (8, 9, 1) have chosen their instinctive center as their preferred way of functioning. The HEART PERSONS (2, 3, 4) have chosen their feeling center as their preferred way of functioning. The HEAD PERSONS (5, 6, 7) have chosen their thinking center as their preferred way of functioning. The difference between (A) GUT PERSONS, (B) HEART PERSONS and (C) HEAD PERSONS may be initially detected by the way each typically enters into a social situation, as follows:

(A) GUT PERSONS enter the situation and say, "Here I am; deal with me."

(B) HEART PERSONS enter the situation and automatically ask, "Are you going to like me or not?"

(C) HEAD PERSONS enter the situation, step back, and ask, "How does this all fit together?"

FIGURE 11 concerns the personality types in the middle of each center, *viz.,* 9, 3, 6. They are called the denial points. Of all the types they are the most likely to deny they have a problem. Their actual problem begins with their lack of proper relationship *to their own preferred center.* They use their preferred center to substitute for the functioning of the other two centers, but to the neglect of using it in its own proper functioning. This means that NINES have a problem in instinctive functioning, THREES in their feeling function and SIXES in the function of their head

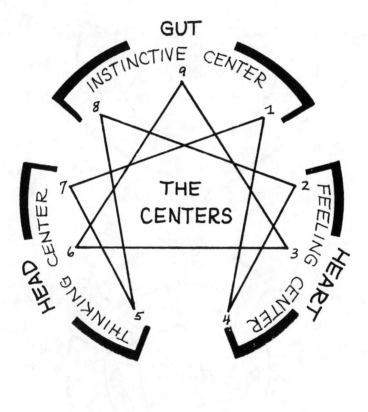

FIGURE 10

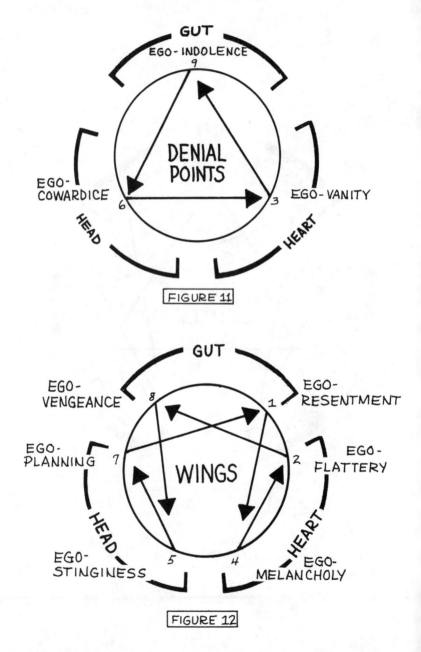

FIGURE 11

FIGURE 12

center.

FIGURE 12 concerns the types which are on the edges of each center on the Enneagram. They are called the wings, and they have *similarities* in personality with the adjacent type in the neighboring center. They deny the functioning of that neighboring center less than they do the center on the opposite side of the Enneagram. Often they may use the proper functioning not only of their preferred center but also the proper functioning of their neighboring center. As regards the other center, which is situated on the opposite side of the Enneagram, they tend to deny its proper functioning and substitute for it the functioning of their preferred center.

The results of these distinctions between *the denial points* and *the wings* is best discussed by taking up the nine types according to (A) GUT PERSONS, (B) HEART PERSONS and (C) HEAD PERSONS, as follows:

(A) GUT PERSONS: 8, 9, 1.

The GUT PERSONS, 8, 9, 1, have chosen their instinctive or moving center as their preferred way of functioning. Typically they enter a situation, plant themselves and say, "Here I am; deal with me." They expect others to focus on them. It is automatic for them to measure themselves in relation to the entire social gathering or situation. They seek control by the power of *just being there.* They seem to say to themselves, "I will be okay in this situation if I simply go with the flow of energy; in that way I will know how to act." Acting by such instinctiveness gives them their sense of dignity and fulfillment. They concentrate on being present and being themselves. Because instinct is built up by past experiences, for them the past tends to dominate. Their energy is also dominated by what should be done, and they have many expectations and demands of others as well as of themselves.

#8. EIGHTS concentrate on being themselves by being strong in relationship to all the others. EIGHTS insist that others deal with them as persons who are strong and rooted in conviction. Being adjacent to the head center, they also are at home in thinking, but they tend to deny their feeling center. Rather than dwelling in their heart center for relationships they use their instinctive center, their own vitality and rootedness, for personal encounter. What results is that they instinctively feel they are relating to another by being assertive whereas actually they may be disrupting the relationship by stepping on the other's toes. They have a real problem entering a feeling experience of tenderness with others and fail to ask the questions characteristic of HEART PERSONS, such as, "Are you going to like me?" or "What do you have need of?" Rather than asking such feeling questions they keep saying, "Deal with me!"

#9. NINES are at the denial point of the gut center on the Enneagram. They tend to use their instinctive center to substitute for the feeling and thinking centers at the price of not living in the proper functioning of the gut center itself. They substitute instinct for feeling, for example, by failing to make new friends and just being content with their habitual friends. Instinct is also used for knowing; they have very limited interests and seem content with a

repetitious kind of knowing through doing the same thing over and over or following the same series of sports events year after year. As regards their instinctive functioning, they seem out of touch with their own inner vitality. They like to live by habit but there is a cap on their instinctive energy to react with vitality to a variety of external stimuli. They often lack a natural and spontaneous reaction to what is happening, and that is one of the main problems which they typically fail to recognize.

#1. ONES are on the wing of the gut center neighboring on the feeling center. They tend to deny their thinking center and substitute for it the way instinct "thinks." This means they fail to ask the questions of HEAD PERSONS, such as, "How does all this go together?" They typically come into a situation with a *bias* in their thinking, making the situation deal with them instead of trying to understand how all the aspects of the situation fit together. ONES characteristically suffer from a lack of objective perspective in their thinking.

(B) HEART PERSONS: 2, 3, 4.

The HEART PERSONS, 2, 3, 4, enter a situation and automatically ask, "Is that person friendly or hostile? . . . Are you going to like me or not?" They also acquire information by asking, "What do you have need of?" They aim at control on the level of how they are with another. They keep asking themselves, "How are others responding to me?" Relationship with others predominates in their concerns. HEART PERSONS process what is needed by another in view of getting a favorable response from the other when they provide something that will please or help.

#2. TWOS are on the wing of the heart center next to the gut center. Although they accept living on a gut level in addition to their preferred heart level, they deny their head center and use the feelings of their heart center as a substitute for the thinking function. They fail to see the value of having a vision of everything and instead narrow their interests to relationships with individual persons. Their usual conversation reveals this narrowness for they mainly talk about people special to them and seem to have little interest for world issues or for any problems beyond their own families. They tend to have a bias also against any abstract thinking, at least to the extent that it is not useful for helping someone they know.

#3. THREES, being at the denial point of the heart center, will substitute their feeling function for the other two centers while having a problem in living on a feeling level. They are notorious for sacrificing the feeling function of personal and family relationships for their success in the business or professional world. They just do not let themselves live deeply in their preferred heart center, and instead they apply its feeling function to substitute for thinking and instinctive behavior. Feeling is used for knowing; they restrict their interests to what will serve their success and thus often suffer from a lack of cultural development of their talents. They fail to recognize knowing as something good in itself; what they strive to know is that which will serve their success, their all-consuming interest. Feeling also is used for instinctive function-

ing; they put on feelings and wear a mask instead of simply letting their person express its instinctive reactions. Their body language portrays an appearance that will cause another to react favorably to what they are selling or promoting.

#4. FOURS, being on the wing of the heart center next to the head center, have a problem with their gut center. They do live on a feeling level and somewhat on a thinking level, but they substitute their feeling function for the gut center. Instead of letting spontaneity happen from instincts they try to make their bodily reactions express a special feeling. They rehearse how they will express themselves instead of just living in their instinctive reactions. They use their feeling for this because they want the expression of themselves to be a way to relate to the other authentically. Thus the uniqueness of their feelings becomes known. The instinctive behavior of the FOUR seems somehow put on, expressing more feeling than actually is in the heart. FOURS tend to wear an artistic mask of bodily movement which keeps others from knowing the real person within.

(C) HEAD PERSONS: 5, 6, 7.

The HEAD PERSONS, 5, 6, 7, have chosen their function of thinking as the most important in being a person. They consider knowing central to their functioning as a person in relationship with the world. They keep asking, "How does this go together?" They look at their whole environment and ask how each part fits with the rest. They do not focus on individuals as HEART PERSONS do; instead, they look at the total situation. They seek to grasp a sense of the total thing and how all the pieces interlock. By experiencing their environment this way they gain a sense of what is happening. With that information they know *how to be in the situation.* They do not boldly enter into the situation and plant themselves there as GUT PERSONS do. They must first know the total situation, and then they know how to fit themselves into it.

As they automatically view the situation, they put themselves in place of others. They try to understand where others are in this thing. They do not center on how they relate to the others but rather on how others simply are in themselves in relationship to the total situation. This enables HEAD PERSONS to enter the lives of others with a spirit of *empathy.* They readily put themselves into the shoes of another by means of the thinking function.

HEAD PERSONS seek control by knowing where everything fits. They are dominated by their ideas, plans and perceptions, for these tell them where everything is. They rely on their thinking and reflection to tell them the whole thing without recognizing the need for any feedback from another. If they themselves think they are okay, then they conclude they are okay. After an experience they will re-play it in their own minds and thereby decide how they will do it the next time.

#5. Being on the wing of the head center, FIVES are also at home in their heart center but they deny the gut center. They put too much self-consciousness into their instinctive life. It is not easy for them to be spontaneous; instead, they tend to be deliberate in their actions and reactions. They first reflect rather than react spontaneously to a new situation. Often they seem very guarded in their reactions. Because memory is an instinctive function and is not under direct control of the mind, they tend to forget people's names. By substituting thinking for the proper functioning of their gut center they may impose on their bodily movements a machine-like regularity. In sports they often are awkward because they use their thinking to replace the natural flow of energy at the gut level needed for consistency of performance and quick reactions.

#6. Because SIXES are at the denial point in the head center, they have a problem living in their preferred head center and use the head center to substitute for the functions proper to the other two centers. They have a problem with *knowing* but deny it. They tend to block out new knowledge which would make life less demanding or threatening. They hold on to the knowledge they have in a very convinced way and consider new knowledge to be threatening because it would add to their responsibilities. The knowledge they have gives them security. It would be unsettling to this security to have new knowledge, for that could cause conflicts with what they already know. They want to live on the head level as the way to have ultimate security, but the content of their knowledge must not change; that would threaten the security their present knowledge gives them. As a result they are reluctant to do serious reading or to attend workshops on new directions in thought. They will dismiss these things as "far out" because they are deemed threatening. They use their head center to substitute for their instinctive and feeling functions. Their bodily movements tend to be ruled by the head center. SIXES consciously conform to the rules their head sees for these movements. By bodily movements they are not expressing themselves but expressing what the head says is to be done because of what is demanded of them. This causes a *rigidity* in behavior, for example, at meetings. What is important to the SIX is that everything be done according to the rules which generally do not vary from meeting to meeting. They also substitute the head function for their heart center. Their sense of responsibility in their work causes them to bypass the question of whether others like them or not, a question asked by HEART PERSONS. The performance of duties is not allowed to be hindered by relating with people on a feeling level during work hours. As a consequence, SIXES can get an enormous amount of work done, and they think they will be loved for the work they get done. It may not occur to them that the feeling level is crucial to love. Parents who are SIXES may think their children should love them because the parents provide material things without the need for the expression of affection or much intimate conversation. SIXES have difficulty in sharing their hearts and tend to explain their lives from the role or responsibility they have been given rather than as a life journey centering on feelings. They see moral issues as a matter of right or wrong according to laws or decisions of authority. They are uncomfortable with gray areas in personal growth. They would not ordinarily say to another that he or she is okay, "because that is where you are at." They think people should simply conform to the standards of a group or else "ship out," even if the group be the family, the church or the nation.

#7. SEVENS are HEAD PERSONS on the wing bordering the gut center. They substitute their thinking function for their heart center. As a consequence they impose their plans on another without much concern for how he or she really feels about the matter. They fail to ask the questions of HEART PERSONS, such as, "Are you friendly to me or hostile?" They simply use their head function of planning to substitute for feeling and presume everyone will enjoy what is being planned. Despite all their effervescence it may not be easy to get really close to them on an intimate level of feeling. They are *party persons* rather than persons who like to cuddle. They like to multiply contact with a number of people rather than spend time with one special other in an intimate setting. Their heads are the center of their lives, and they think that by planning enjoyable activities they can please everyone.

PART THREE
Overcoming One's Compulsion

5. *ACTING AGAINST THE COMPULSION*

Anyone under a compulsion needs help. That help can come from three sources: oneself, others and God. Those with compulsive personalities can help themselves by understanding their problem and working out a corresponding solution through their own efforts. They can get help from others, especially from a close friend who understands their compulsion and consequently can help to free them from its influence. They can also obtain help from God who offers salvation to all through faith.

All three forms of help are aspects of *redemption*. The term "redemption" is derived from paying a ransom to release captives from slavery. Compulsions cause a kind of slavery. They are prevailing inner drives preventing persons from living in the freedom of fully integrated humanness. A ransom or price must be paid for this liberation. Jesus paid the price of redemption for all human persons through his passion and death, but he does not do the ransoming alone. He calls each person to be willing to lose his or her life in order to find it (Mt 16:25). He unites his disciples in friendship to minister to one another with his love (Jn 15:16f). He also continually insists on the need to live by faith if one is to be saved by God's direct action, i.e., if one is to enter the Kingdom of God.

This chapter on *acting against the compulsion* concerns the *efforts* that need to be made to move to self from being compulsive to being "redeemed." These efforts do not change a person from one personality type on the Enneagram to another personality type or in any way diminish one's identification with the personality type which developed in early childhood. That same personality type will endure throughout the redemption process, even though there can be a *marvelous transformation* touching *all the underlying causes* of the compulsion. Each personality type may be compared to a tree, which characteristically retains its basic structure determined in the early stages of growth but bursts into blossom and bears much fruit, giving it a singular beauty and making its life bountiful for many.

The "ransom" for redeeming the self needs to be *paid* by all three sources of help: by oneself, by others and by God. The price paid by oneself is indicated by a pathway of "moving against the arrows" in the Enneagram. This is symbolic of the kind of experience such a personal effort is. It is an *agere contra,* an "acting against." One moves contrary to the inner inclination of the compulsion. The Enneagram provides a clear "map" of the direction for each personality type.

The price others pay for one's redemption from compulsion will be reflected on by asking how a friend can help each personality type become more free. The price paid by God has already been accomplished in Jesus. How to apply this to one's compulsion will be discussed in Chapter 6. It will concern the topic of *con-version*, seen in its three aspects of intellectual conversion, affective conversion and instinctual conversion. The intellectual conversion pertains to moving from the "trap" to the "Holy idea"; the affective conversion deals with virtues healing the passions; the instinctual conversion concerns discernment of spirits which is especially helpful in the spiritual maturation of each personality type.

Moving Against the Arrows

Self-help in being redeemed centers on "moving against the arrows" of compulsion. This involves moving against the arrow by moving *toward the pride* of the other personality type. FIGURE 13 shows the arrows of compulsion along with the pride of each personality type. FIGURE 14 portrays Dunne's general pattern of movement in moving against the arrows according to the three preferred *modes of behavior:* (1) AGGRESSIVE, (2) DEPENDENT and (3) WITH-DRAWING.

(1) AGGRESSIVE TYPES: 8, 3, 1.

The AGGRESSIVE TYPES, 8, 3, 1, *act against* their compulsion to aggressivity by moving against the arrows toward dependent behavior. Instead of being on the offensive against social reality, they become more accepting of the world as it is.

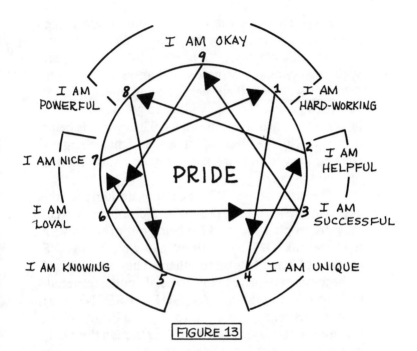

FIGURE 13

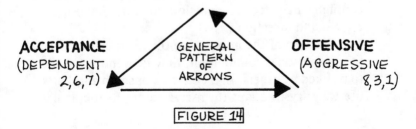

FIGURE 14

#8.

EIGHTS move against their compulsion to aggressiveness by taking on the pride of the TWO, who
characteristically says, "I am helpful." TWOS see
social reality as full of needy customers and seek out
people who need their help. Seeing themselves as
generous givers, they are willing to go even as far as
laying down their lives for others. Their pride is being
important in the lives of others and having many
friends. They dislike violence, whether it hurts another
or themselves.

The pride of the TWO is a strong antidote for the
aggressiveness of EIGHTS, who are noted for stepping on people's toes and for being out of touch with
tenderness. EIGHTS benefit by taking on the TWO'S
attitude of being helpful to others. They are softened
by becoming attentive to the needs of another especially through friendship. As GUT PERSONS they
characteristically come into a situation, plant
themselves and say, "Here I am," as though the whole
world is supposed to focus on them. By moving
against the arrow of their compulsion and moving
toward the TWO, EIGHTS are actually attending to
their heart center, which inclines them to see the other
before they see themselves. Instead of always measur-
ing themselves in relationship with the other, they try
through their feeling function to win the other's
esteem and affection.

Because of the importance the heart center gives
to interpersonal communion, they take more trouble
to be liked by others. In their intrusions into another's
life they try to adapt themselves more to the actual

needs of the person and what is acceptable rather than simply impose themselves.

#3.

THREES move against their compulsion of aggressive behavior by taking on the pride of the SIX, who characteristically says, "I am loyal" (to the norms of the group). SIXES, therefore, are faithful to relationships within the group. This fidelity gives them an acute sensitivity to the wishes of those in authority.

By moving toward the SIX, THREES take on a greater loyalty to their whole group of co-workers and make group norms binding on themselves. This prevents them from falling into their tendency to use the group for their own ends and advancement. They also need to take on the *conscience* of the SIX as formed by external authority. THREES tend to disregard laws and social norms in their quest to achieve their own ends. They take advantage of others, often through deceit. To avoid this lack of personal integrity, they benefit by submitting their business activities, as well as their private lives, to the moral code and civil laws. By taking on the self-image of loyal and obedient citizens and members of society, they move away from their compulsion to be successful at any cost. It is also important for THREES to take pride in being faithful and devoted to their family relationships because they tend to identify their lives with their ambitions.

To move toward the SIX also means that THREES take on characteristics of HEAD PERSONS. They benefit by trying to see objectively how everything in society fits together and how they relate to the social whole and the common good. Compulsively they seek to build up their own kingdom in competition with others. They need to see with their head center that they are called to be a part of society through cooperation and a spirit of interdependence. This helps them broaden their loyalty to society itself rather than live for their own enterprise, and gives them a sense of satisfaction in the achievements of the whole human community even though these are not their own achievements.

#1.

ONES act against their compulsive aggressiveness by moving toward the pride of the SEVEN, who characteristically says, "I am nice." SEVENS are optimistic and enthusiastic about the future. They approach persons and situations without guile or suspicion. They share their contagious enjoyment of life by telling personal-interest stories in an entertaining manner. They focus on the bright side of life and talk away pain and tension.

It is healthy for ONES to enjoy life the way SEVENS do. ONES need to become less serious. It helps them to go to silly parties and be part of the fun. They need to let "the sun of life" shine on them. When they become fun-loving, they are more teasable and playful, which aids them to accept themselves and the world as it is.

In moving toward the SEVEN, ONES also benefit by becoming more like HEAD PERSONS, thereby approaching reality in a more objective and

dispassionate way. ONES resent the world and think
nothing is the way it should be. It is a mistake to constantly find fault and never be satisfied with the way
things are. ONES are often obsessed with post-
mortems: "Was that okay? . . . What was wrong
with that? . . . How did it go wrong?" They need to
move from taking the offensive against social reality
to accepting things as they are. This means ONES need
to live more in their thinking center, letting reality
speak to them as it is, rather than crusading to set it
right. By perceiving objectively the good already present around them, they can move from worry, fussing
and anxiety. Taking on the penchant of the SEVEN to
amuse and entertain others by talking a lot and telling
funny stories and anecdotes, they defuse their pent-up
anger and fit better into their environment. Like
SEVENS, they need to concentrate on seeing good in
everything rather than being picky about deficiencies.

(2) DEPENDENT TYPES: 2, 6, 7.
The DEPENDENT TYPES, 2, 6, 7, *act against*
their compulsion of adapting to circumstances when
they move against the arrow toward withdrawing
behavior. Instead of conforming to social reality they
become more defensive.

#2.

TWOS act against their compulsive dependency
on another's approval by moving toward the pride of
the FOUR, who characteristically says, "I am
unique" (and therefore misunderstood). FOURS are
romantics and see themselves surrounded by beautiful

things which only they can fully appreciate. With their passion for spontaneity and simplicity they often turn to nature because it is simple, individual and fresh. Unable to express their profound feelings they tend toward ritualization, dramatization and the theatrical where they strive to express themselves in a fullness of originality and uniqueness.

By moving toward the FOUR, TWOS benefit by striving to express themselves as very special and unique persons having deep feelings of joy and sorrow. They thus become more free of their ego fixation to be simply helpers without needs. Taking on the pride of the FOUR causes them to recognize their deep need to be appreciated for their own gifts and unique life story rather than for what they do for another. It aids them to have a sense of their own unique lovableness because they are especially sensitive and affective. Instead of always adapting themselves to the needs of another, they withdraw more to reflect on their feelings and rehearse how to express authentically who they really are as persons. This helps them grow as HEART PERSONS who are able to share their feelings with others in intimacy.

#6.

SIXES act against their compulsive dependency of conforming to outside reality by moving against the arrow to take on the pride of the NINE, who characteristically says, "I am okay." NINES are seldom upset by inner conflict, and they insist that those around them live in peace. They make excellent reconcilers. They are naturally objective, impartial and dispassionate and like to get everyone settled.

By moving toward the NINE, SIXES give greater authority *to their own gut instincts* and thus become more confident and less anxious about what others think. They need the NINE'S inner quietude. This comes by living less in their head center and more in their gut reactions to situations. They become more like GUT PERSONS, less cautious and circumspect about trying new things. Instead of asking, "How do I fit into the total situation?" they let go of their apprehensiveness by saying, "Here I am; deal with me." SIXES need the confidence of GUT PERSONS that by going with the flow they will be okay as persons. They trust their inner instincts to react adequately to situations as they happen. To do this they need to tone down their super-responsibility. Compulsively they make too big a deal out of what some authority has said or of some traditional way of doing something as though such external norms were ends in themselves. It is healthy for SIXES to take on the NINE'S spontaneous attitude that what is really important is harmony between persons and within oneself. The interior conflicts of SIXES are often projected onto others. SIXES exaggerate the importance of certain external observances to the detriment of the greater value of peace. To move toward the pride of the NINE means that SIXES form their consciences by the values of peace, love and harmony rather than by a strict obedience to external norms and customs.

#7.

SEVENS *act against* their compulsive dependency on pleasure by moving against the arrow to take on the pride of the FIVE, who characteristically says, "I am knowing." Instead of seeking to be in harmony with external social reality, SEVENS become healthier by withdrawing from others in the manner of the FIVE. FIVES crave knowledge for its own sake. They distance themselves to view the panorama. They think systematically and produce generalizations from a comprehensive examination of every possible aspect of a given issue.

By taking on a more reflective life in the manner of the FIVE, SEVENS come to face themselves in relation to outer reality with greater objectivity, instead of projecting their own optimism onto reality, which they often do in a superficial way. It is healthy for them to become more observant and empathetic, to put themselves in the shoes of others and to delight in coming to know reality as it really is in all its complexity, rather than to pretend everything is "nice." Knowing reality more objectively through observation and reflection enables them to get in touch with their own "inner well" of wisdom, which can unite them on a deeper level with other persons. To become more reflective gives them a greater tolerance for pain and for tasks which are laborious but nonetheless meaningful and worthwhile to accomplish. A withdrawing and reflective behavior characteristic of the FIVE helps SEVENS become less "flighty"; they see that what is important is not that everything be pleasant, but that *they are a part of reality.*

(3) WITHDRAWING TYPES: 5, 9, 4.

The WITHDRAWING TYPES, 5, 9, 4, *act against* the compulsiveness of their withdrawing behavior by moving against the arrow to take on a more assertive behavior. In this way they move from defensiveness into being on the *offensive* toward social reality.

#5.

FIVES move against their compulsive attitude of defensiveness by taking on the pride of the EIGHT who characteristically says, "I am powerful." EIGHTS take pride in being strong persons, in not being stepped on or taken advantage of. They see through the pretentious and hypocritical. They gravitate naturally to power, to being on top. They see the solution to problems as an exercise of power. They know how to use their strength to confront and debunk situations and persons. EIGHTS lust for intensity in life.

By moving toward the EIGHT, FIVES make use of their *power* with others rather than withdrawing. FIVES, however, never become assertive the way the EIGHT is assertive, but greater aggressiveness is a healthy direction for them to take. They benefit by living more in their instinctive center. Often they are awkward with their bodies because they live too much in their heads. The body has its own wisdom and can react spontaneously to situations much faster than a person can through reflective thought and deliberate action. Often FIVES miss opportunities to elicit more truth from a situation. They are too slow to react because they fail to let themselves live on a gut level of reaction in words, gestures and feelings. Such gut-level reaction becomes more available to them when they are assertive even though this may not feel right to them. It frees them to use the power they have as persons and causes others to respond to them and their vision. This strengthening of the "inner muscles" of their personality gives them a better sense of themselves, which they direly need. Even though they are among the types which say, "I am bigger than the world," they feel inadequate and empty inside in face of the fresh challenges of life. By trusting in the inner wisdom of their instinctive center and making others deal with them, they become more creative.

Involvement lessens their need for huge stores of knowledge before they move into the world. EIGHTS have an instinct to react first and reflect later. FIVES are long-practised at reflection, but its treasures are greater when they stop denying the importance of gut reactions. They avoid others to protect their ideas from theft and abuse. It is healthy for them to take on the EIGHT'S willingness to get a bit bruised in the battles of life as well as to allow themselves permission to be more instinctive and earthy.

#9.

NINES will come to life by moving toward the pride of the THREE, who characteristically says, "I am successful." THREES equate activity and achievement with life. They are competitive; their feelings rarely interfere with their ambition. They like tangible signs of progress. They recruit teams and direct all toward a common objective. Because THREES are enthusiastic and precise in advertizing their own image, others are persuaded to buy their goal. Their achievements are often admired by society.

By moving toward the THREE, NINES act against their compulsion to withdraw from life and move against the arrow to a more assertive behavior toward social reality. It is healthy for them to set goals and move toward them. They need to get things done and to take on a self-image that they are efficient persons.

For NINES to take the attitude of being a self-starter in imitation of the THREE, they need to find resources within themselves by recognizing their innate gifts. They are aided to do this by becoming more like HEART PERSONS who characteristically ask how to become likable and lovable, involved in personal relationships on a feeling level. Often it happens that NINES grew up with unaffectionate parents. They came to take it for granted that they were not loved and that they should not expect to be loved. In a spirit of resignation they devised a strategy to defend themselves against the pain and hurt of being deprived of care. They said, "So I am neglected; well, life is not that big a deal anyway; people make a lot of fuss over nothing; life is not that important." By learning to live more in their heart center, NINES begin to look for personal love to awaken the neglected life of the heart. By the experience of being loved they begin to love themselves and see themselves as worthwhile and gifted. Although they cannot cause anyone to love them, they can move toward a much greater concern for matters of the heart, cultivate their appearance before others and seek to get others to respond to them. This means they must take the initiative in cultivating new interests which will make them *more interesting and attractive* as persons. Once interpersonal love becomes a reality for them, they may awaken to find life more important than they ever dreamed. The impact of past lack of affection can be lessened and the question, "What is life?" becomes a new fascination to them.

#4.

FOURS move from their compulsion of withdrawal by taking on the pride of the ONE who characteristically says, "I am hard-working." ONES feel most alive when making an effort to counteract evil, disorder and error. They are relentless in pursuit of the perfection that eludes them.

They interrupt and interfere with reality to correct it. They see themselves as defenders of the truth with the generous intent of teaching others for their betterment. They are attracted to activities that promise self-improvement. Their greatest pride is in how hard they try to do good and be good.

By moving toward the ONE, FOURS abandon their defensive stance toward the world and become more assertive. Instead of lamenting about how they have been misunderstood, they voice more criticism of what is outside themselves and make efforts to change the way things are. By taking on some of the ONE'S idealism and quest for a more perfect world, they get a better sense of themselves and see their refinement and sensitivity as gifts for the betterment of others. By moving against the world like a ONE, FOURS focus more on urging others to improvement rather than dwelling on their own specialness. In taking on the assertive criticism so characteristic of the ONE, FOURS never become ONES but simply tend to move out of their own compulsion by becoming more *involved* with external reality and seeing themselves as dedicated to honesty, directness and hard work. This means that they learn to live more in their neglected instinctive center by making others respond to them and their values.

Getting Help from a Friend

Another resource for redeeming the compulsive self is help from a friend who knows the compulsion and has the skill to respond to it in a redeeming way. Some suggestions of how to respond to each personality type are as follows:

#1. ONES are perfectionists. They are rigorous in over-criticism of themselves and others. Often their compulsion catches them on some one point and they overwork it. A friend is more helpful to them *by asking them questions than by telling them things.* The friend shows interest in their personal gifts and helps them get started in new use of their talents. They need to be listened to on their own wavelength; otherwise they say they are not heard. A friend listens by taking seriously what they bring up again and again; he or she says, "This is really important to you because you keep repeating it." ONES should be encouraged to laugh. They benefit amazingly by acknowledging their own foibles as funny. *Teasing* is a natural way of

enlightening them about being overly serious. They like to be teased but the way they return teasing may be more pointed than light-hearted.

#2. TWOS think they are independent but actually they are dependent on appreciation for their service. They are helped by a friend *to own their personal need.* A friend calls them to be aware of their feelings and assures them that it is okay to have needs by saying, "It is great to know you also have needs for that makes you human like the rest of us." A friend should beware of *using* TWOS; it is so easy to get them to fulfill all one's petty needs. They run and get anything and everything without argument. What they need is affection; they need to be nurtured. They do not ask for affection because they do not like to ask for what they need. They are not helped out of their compulsion by being patted on the back for all the little things they do or by being fawned over. A friend refuses to affirm their compulsion to get approval by what they do to help. Instead of loving them for doing what pleases, love them for who they are. The time to give them a hug is not when they have just performed a service but when they are genuinely themselves.

#3. THREES are helped by being affirmed as persons rather than for what they do. A friend helps them be themselves by accepting, affirming and delighting in their personal qualities. They need to be told they are successes just by being who they are. They also need to be helped to face their own failures, mistakes and frustrations with realism. A friend refuses to speak of some failure they have had as somehow a "grand success." It is important for THREES to accept failure for what it is, as part of what it means to

accept life. A friend says, "I feel more at one with you when you join the rest of the human race." When THREES are over-emphasizing competition with others, they need to be called to a greater balance of outlook, perhaps through a gentle understatement. They are often unaware of how their feelings are affecting them. When they make over-positive or over-enthusiastic statements they should be questioned about the statements and called to ownership for what they say. In that way a friend can be a gift to them by mentioning what they tend to slide over. THREES have a compulsion to substitute quantity for quality; they try for too many successes. Perhaps as children they were never loved separately from their achievements, so they came to take pride only in their success. They look at themselves from the outside as though they *are* their achievements. They need to be shown that their real worth is in themselves and not in the multiplication of successes. A friend's love for them simply as persons replaces the false love they experienced earlier in life, which caused them to cling to their compulsion for success as a measure of their worth.

#4. FOURS over-reason everything. They keep asking the eternal "Why?" A friend helps them by calling them to own their own strength as they are without going to extremes. They are helped by a friend sharing with them his or her own perspectives. Here the relationship is key, for they will listen to a different view only if they feel the other understands them. For them, that is what having a friend means. Since they love to absorb information, a friend has a real opportunity to tell them what they need to hear to be more

free, namely, how ordinary things in life can be appreciated.

#5. FIVES are helped by a friend to come out of their cave and be something more than perpetual observers of everything. They can out-wait anybody, so to wait for them to come out on their own may mean to wait a very long time! Knowing that FIVES have worlds within, a friend keeps inviting them to make more use of the power they have. This is to call them out of stinginess to share themselves and make what they know beneficial to others. They should be invited into activity and to try something new with their friend. In effect, the friend needs to put them on stage and say, "Dance!"

#6. Because the greatest obstacle of growth for SIXES is their own *fear*, a friend helps them by calling them to test their courage in various ways. It is important not to give advice to them. They need to be encouraged to make their own decisions. A good question for the friend to ask is, "What do *you* really want to do?" The friend then affirms them in whatever decision they make and stays with them as they try to carry it out, even if it does not turn out right. Patience is needed in helping them come to a personal decision. If they are in a group and are the first to be asked to make a decision, their compulsion will lead them to choose what they believe the others want. They need to be given time to get things clarified in their minds before responding. They also need to be helped to get in touch with their fears. They deal with fear on a daily basis. When they are given authority, they are afraid of any dissenting voices and tend to become *authoritarian* to show others who is boss. A friend

helps them see other constructive ways of exercising leadership and become more aware that responsibility need not rest only on their shoulders but can be shared with others in a trusting way.

#7. SEVENS are dreamers. Their plans for the future cause them to become over-enthusiastic, and the actual experience of carrying out the plans does not come up to their expectations. A friend calls them to greater accountability for their dreams by saying, "This is what you said and this is what you did." They are encouraged to make real only some of their plans because their total planning usually outstrips the possible. As regards their penchant to avoid pain, a friend says it is not necessary that everything be rosy and there is nothing wrong in expecting that life will include some hard spots. It is important that SEVENS not be rescued from the bad consequences of their non-action.

A friend helps them by letting them pick up the pieces of their own procrastination. They are to be called on their neglect and reminded that once they have made a plan it is expected that they will follow through on its implementation. SEVENS need to be made aware of the pain and trouble they cause another by their neglect because compulsively they tend to block this out of their consciousness. A friend tells them how their procrastination or non-action has hurt another. Their motivation of wanting everyone to be happy can help them in the future to be more reliable. In any case, by calling them to account, a friend aids them in being more in touch with reality as it is instead of smoothing over everything.

#8. EIGHTS are seekers of strict justice. They at-

tack something with full force and miss how others feel. They benefit by being told by a friend how others felt or even how the friend felt. Since they act as EIGHTS towards a friend as well as towards others, the friend needs to be a strong person to make the friendship a real sharing in life. He or she needs to be able to come back to the EIGHT with such statements as, "Do you know how I felt when you said that?" EIGHTS will respect anyone taking responsibility for his or her own feelings. It is wise, however, not to take on the aggressiveness of EIGHTS in responding to them. A genuine *gentleness* is much more helpful, both to the EIGHT and to the relationship, than an aggressive retort. EIGHTS love a fight and defend themselves self-righteously even when it is a close friend who complains abrasively of having been hurt by what the EIGHT said or did. EIGHTS put the fault on the other; they were just being themselves and the other tripped over them. They need to learn how to respond on a feeling level and also they need to hear how strongly they come across to others. A friend needs to be unafraid of them, not backing off from them in any way, but gently *calling them to their tender side.* There is more than one way to speak the truth; arrogance is not the only way to clear the air and communicate effectively. In relating to EIGHTS, a friend needs to be prepared for strong, sudden reactions from them. Often they feel they have spoken the truth others do not want to hear. A friend also needs to expect that the first response EIGHTS make to a new suggestion is "no," but later they may soften and change their answer to "yes."

#9. NINES are non-conformists. They don't

agree with how the world is, so they tend not to operate in it. When they begin to discover how they are as persons they generally don't like what they find and this causes them to be inactive. A friend helps NINES by calling them to take a stand and to have a sense of making a difference in the world. It may be mystifying to know how to call out NINES; they seem so lacking in energy and enthusiasm. A friend begins by accepting them however they are and then expressing belief in them by inviting them to join in activities and holding them accountable for the part they have.

NINES are like a pump that needs to be primed. They need someone else to get something going and then invite them to join. They do want to be stimulated by others, and thus they will tend to respond when another takes the initiative.

6. CONVERSION

Besides seeking redemption of the compulsed self through one's own resources by moving against the arrow of compulsion, and through help from a friend who understands, what remains *crucial* for a deep inner healing of the self is a *direct personal relationship with God.* Such a relationship is best described as *holy abandonment* because this is the only adequate and true way to be in union with God as creative SOURCE of all and thus as redemptive RESTORER of all. The act of abandonment to God can influence and rectify all the energies of one's being, beginning with the head center. Abandonment to God is first of all an *intellectual conversion,* a way of seeing all reality and how one is a part of it according to the divine plan. Intellectual conversion leads to *affective conversion*, which concerns the heart center. Following upon affective conversion there may be a conversion of the instinctual energies of human nature.

Conversion occurs because being rooted in God through faith—accepting God as God—results in the development of a reliance on God's power and love in one's life. Through this reliance on God the less conscious parts of one's being are trusted to respond from one's inner well of energy without the self feeling threatened by some loss of control or other disaster.

Intellectual Conversion: The Holy Ideas

In the Enneagram, intellectual conversion is designated as the movement from *the trap to the holy idea.* A trap is an habitual way of acting derived from ego consciousness. It involves getting *caught* in a pattern of behavior that is compulsive. To be so caught in the trap is to be un-free. It stymies personal growth. Simply to say, "This how I am," and to accept being that way while all the time being caught in the trap is to *evade responsibility for one's actions.* It is to fail to choose something other than the compulsion as a way of life. The compulsion is a consequence of the ego consciousness saying to the world, "I do not need you to be fully a person." It represents a strategy set up by the ego for self-salvation.

By bringing in the *holy idea* which is basic to abandonment to God, the self is moved out of this defense strategy of self-salvation and opened to accept *a need for God* in order to achieve personal fulfillment. This is an opening to TRUTH and it is crucial to being set free from ego fixation.

Enneagram theory affixes a distinct "holy idea" to each personality type. This recognizes that each type has a distinctive trap or "false idea" which needs to be exposed and redeemed by an unconditional reliance on God in lieu of relying only on the resources of the self. FIGURE 15 depicts the Enneagram according to the nine *traps* which are to be replaced by the nine *holy ideas* depicted in FIGURE 16.

The commentary which follows will simply follow the numerical order around the Enneagram from 1 to 9.

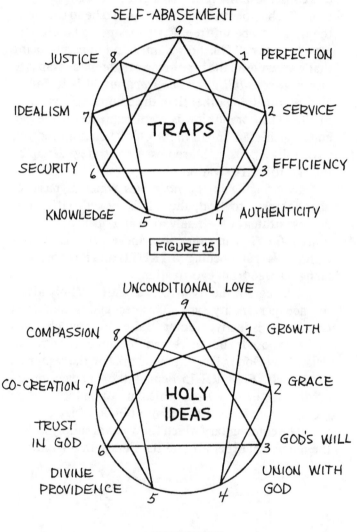

FIGURE 15

FIGURE 16

#1.

The trap for ONES is their idea of *perfection,* which is an obsession for them. Bothered by the smallest imperfection, they strive for an unattainable ideal perfection. Nothing they do satisfies them so they constantly find fault. Reality *is not* perfect! They try ever harder and become increasingly impatient. For them what counts is the *now.* They are not process people.

The holy idea of *growth* can release ONES from their trap of perfection. It recognizes that God governs the world in an evolutionary way. According to God's revealed design for the universe all creation is in the process of becoming. This reveals that God's way of achieving betterment in the world consists in *process.* The real perfection of creatures involves their being in the process of becoming. To exist and to be alive is a call from God to grow and become mature. The living organism at any stage in its development can be said to be "perfect" inasmuch as it is at a certain stage in its growth. Even mistakes can be counted as serving this process of maturation, as something a person needs to go through. Not to make any mistakes could be an indication that one is simply not trying anything new in order to grow.

For ONES to abandon themselves to God involves their accepting God's way of designing creatures to grow in gradual steps. It means accepting one's creaturehood under God. This can lead ONES to see that it is okay to have loose ends in what happens and that imperfections and mistakes are all part of becoming a person. Holiness itself is seen as a pro-

cess of growth rather than as attaining some norm of
being complete and correct. In this way ONES can live
in greater peace and serenity concerning how things
actually are and rely on God's way of governing the
universe through a process of becoming instead of imposing their own idea of perfection.

#2.

The trap of the TWOS is their idea of *service.*
Because of this idea of service they think themselves
totally selfless, whereas they are very dependent on the
expressed appreciation, attention and affection of
those they serve. Their help always has strings attached, and they will reproach those who do not give
or love in return. They play on the sympathy of
another saying, "How can you do this to me after all I
have done for you?" They seldom directly ask for
something, but indirectly they attempt to make the
other want to give it to them. When others fail to respond to this manipulation, they feel taken advantage
of. This means they may be helping others more out of
their own need to be appreciated than out of a sincere
concern for people. They will flatter others and serve
their superfluous needs. They offer over-effusive
compliments, rescue others against their will, give
unasked-for advice and unctuous care—all out of their
own need for approval and acceptance. This trap of
service makes them jealous and possessive. They have
much unowned anger because they do not feel appreciated.

The holy idea of *grace* can release TWOS from
their idea of service. For them abandonment to God

means above all the recognition that there is *no way to win God's love:* it is always a *free gift.* God loved them before they performed any service. It was out of love that God brought them into existence and out of that love that they are saved. This love comes from God's free choice; it cannot be deserved or won in any way. It is simply given as grace. It is this grace—God's "prevenient" love—that makes them lovable and gives them meaning and worth. Because they are trapped in their idea of service, TWOS tend to relate to God the way they relate to others, i.e., by doing something to please. By heeding the call to believe in God's grace they can have a conversion—a change in attitude—such that they accept God as loving them because of *who* they are and not for what they have done in service. This frees them to begin to accept themselves as already unconditionally *loved.* As a consequence they may stop their desperate attempts to win love from others to satisfy what was a craving for approval.

Such an intellectual conversion in TWOS probably is the fruit of quiet prayer. They naturally find such prayer difficult since it seems like "doing nothing" and by compulsion they want to be always doing for another. To spend time alone with God is to do something *for themselves* in order to receive the grace they need. Because it is their compulsion not to do something just for themselves, quiet prayer in solitude will probably happen only when they begin to take account of their needs and thereby become willing to expend time and energy on themselves for their own personal well-being.

#3.

The trap for THREES is their idea of *efficiency,* namely, that they think they have to be efficient to be worthwhile and that this is also true for other people. They make life consist simply in achievements in competition with others. As a consequence, they are always looking for a quicker or more profitable way of doing things, even to the point that they actually become less efficient. This quest for efficiency is tied in with their ambitious plans, goals and expectations. All time is valuable for them, chiefly in being used to achieve the objectives of their own enterprises, and the purpose of life itself is to get ahead.

The holy idea of *God's will* can release THREES from the trap they are caught in because they are obsessed with efficiency. The main way for THREES to abandon themselves to God is to put their lives and their energies under God's government of the world and to recognize the world as belonging to God. It is to accept God as the "Great Administrator" over all creation. By holy abandonment THREES offer their lives in service to God's goals, objectives and action plans. They come to see they are to live in happy submission to God's way of working in the world and to make their own plans for success not as absolutes but as relative to God's plans, which may only gradually become known. A failure in their own achievements is not necessarily a failure in God's plans for them. Even if their failure is something not actually willed but only "permitted" by God, it remains God's will that good come out of the failure.

Trust in God and the divine will is an antidote for

their excessive spirit of competition since in God's Administration there is providential concern for the activities of all other individuals and groups in the world. God's Kingdom is built through the activities of many, all expressing their special God-given talents and trying to use them according to the opportunities they have. When THREES accept the whole world as properly God's Kingdom and see that they are called to have a part in its upbuilding along with many others, they are more able to rejoice in the accomplishments of another who otherwise would be considered as a competitor or even a hindrance to their own achievements.

#4.

FOURS are trapped by their idea of *authenticity*, which they see as something they can achieve by themselves if they remain in touch with all that has happened to them, and they keep practicing how to express their deepest feelings in their personalities. As a result they keep mulling over the feelings they have from past experiences to the detriment of being able to live in the present in a relaxed and satisfied way. They get so preoccupied with all that makes them special because of their past experiences that they feel no one can understand what they have gone through. This makes them somehow unreal as persons, as though they were aristocrats in exile, putting on airs. They do sense they are never quite themselves, but they believe that they will become truly authentic once they finally begin to live their "real lives."

The holy idea of *union with God* can release

FOURS from their obsession with authenticity. It is only through union with God that a person truly becomes himself or herself in a unique and striking way. God creates each human person to be unique and irreplaceable[26] and through divine providence works with all the joys and sorrows of that person's life to bring out that uniqueness as a special gift of God to the world at that point in history. Whatever tragedy and lost opportunities have been in a person's life can still serve to bring out that unique gift to others. FOURS abandon themselves to God by making their lives a journey to God. By yearning for union with God above all else, they see all life experiences as growthful. What becomes most important is allowing each experience to be a means to grow in union with God. This can happen only by living in the present because God can be met only in the *now*-moment. By living their lives as a response to God in whatever is presented in the present moment FOURS are freed from living in the nostalgia of past tragedy. They accept God's reign over their life experiences as the way to attain the kind of originality they are intended by God to have. By accepting abandonment to God as a way of life they discover in themselves a new creativity in self-expression which spontaneously comes forth from them in response to life as it is, even on an ordinary day-by-day basis. God's gifts in the circumstances we experience never do make life merely ordinary or routine; each moment, through the hand of God and the divine presence in it, is what has been called "the sacrament of the present moment."[27]

#5.

FIVES are trapped by the insatiable quest for *knowledge.* They find life fascinating to know from a distance but too terrifying for personal involvement. Feeling like abandoned orphans they withdraw from others and meet their personal needs through thought and reflection. They equate perception with experience, ideating rather than feeling and acting. Quantity of information replaces depth of experience. Ask them how they feel and they will tell you what they think. They compartmentalize everything, viewing even their own lives as a series of distinct events. The most difficult action for FIVES is to request help; they are compelled to find all their resources within themselves. Weak interpersonal relationships make commitment and loyalty problematic.

The holy idea of *divine providence* releases FIVES from the trap of their idea that knowledge is most important and that they have to withdraw from others to attain it. Divine providence means that God acts in our lives to take care of all our needs. Included in these needs is whatever we need to know in order to function well. This idea that what we need to know will be provided by God through what happens in our lives makes FIVES more willing to get involved with life rather than just to watch it and reflect on it. By getting involved in persons and events around them they begin to allow life to be the teacher God intends it to be for them. They trust that God provides the opportunity through events for them to be prepared adequately for each circumstance and provides assistance to them in their actual involvement with others and with the tasks they undertake. Such an idea of divine providence offers an intellectual conversion to FIVES. They find themselves invited to make a leap of faith, trusting in a practical way that God will provide for all the needs they have in order to do things well.

It is only in becoming involved socially that they know what really is going on, for life itself can be known only by personal involvement. This makes it a "mystery."[28] Reading books or observing what is happening never brings a person to know the true mystery of life, the mystery of "being in communion." By letting life be their teacher through social involvement FIVES will also be able to get in touch with the spirit of the times which awakens in human aspirations all over the world as though persons are being taught the same thing at the same moment in history. It is as though the same underground spring is feeding the deep wells of many persons. By becoming involved with others through the gift of themselves FIVES discover within themselves wisdom they never dreamed they had. The indwelling Spirit of God makes responses from within them to the varied circumstances they meet. They come to experience a wisdom hardly mentioned by books but which is directly written on human hearts.

SIXES are trapped by their idea of *security*, which is based on obedience to authority, persons or norms. Loyalty to a leader promises protection from their self-doubt and indecision. Fear inhibits their freedom to become self-actualized. Instead they are over-cautious and blocked in communication and action. Orthodoxy masquerades as courage, authoritarianism as decisiveness. When living up to the expectations they have introjected becomes intolerable,

SIXES rebel by projecting their resentment and deviance on others. SIXES perceive a questioning of their ideas or procedures as a personal attack because they overidentify with their own thoughts. They feel themselves to be personifications of the groups or institutions to which they belong; therefore, criticism of group values is considered a personal affront.

The holy idea of *trust in God* can release SIXES from the trap of their own idea of security. Trust is our response to God's offering of self through Jesus to believers as our basic security, as the rock on which to build our lives. This security based on trust in God involves the "covenant" of divine adoption. Through this holy idea of trust in God SIXES will see they have come from God and are going back to God; nothing can hurt them, not even death, because God loves them as children. Much of the gospel message in the New Testament, especially as found in Paul's epistles, seems formulated specifically to free persons trapped by the compulsion of the SIX. This compulsion looks for ultimate security in religion as an institution of observances and external laws rather than in the security called salvation in God's covenant of divine adoption, which precedes any external observances of commandments or customs. For SIXES, to abandon themselves to God means trusting God's parental love as the ultimate security for their lives.

#7.

SEVENS are trapped by their idea of *idealism*, which causes them to avoid and deny whatever is painful. They are on a head trip, thinking about how nice things were or will be, rather than living and acting in the present—the real world. They are compelled to dispel gloom with their habitual smile. They experience the joy of an event in its planning, so they often fail to actualize their plans. They find everything interesting, especially if they can talk about it.

The holy idea of *co-creation* can release SEVENS from the trap of their idea of idealism. Co-creation means working with God according to the way the Creator works in the world to bring about that which is better. This way of working in our actual world is revealed through the paschal mystery of Jesus which shows that new life follows from dying to oneself and joy follows from pain endured with patience. Jesus likened the coming of God's Kingdom to the process of giving birth through labor pains (Jn 16:20-22). To suffer *for something* is to be like a seed dying to itself now to yield later a rich harvest of joy (Jn 12:24). St. Paul saw all creation at present in labor pains which are a sign of the coming of a glorious future (Rm 8:18-25). This idea of co-creation through the paschal mystery leads SEVENS to accept the details of work needed to implement their plans to make life better. To get involved in God's creative process has the necessary consequence of accepting suffering, hard labor and disappointments. Instead of trying to escape such pain, as SEVENS do in their idealism, they accept carrying their cross as the necessary price to be paid for achieving any good. This constitutes the chief way they abandon themselves to God.

#8.

EIGHTS are trapped by their idea of *justice.* They are over-sensitive to the issue of upholding their own rights to preserve their personal dignity and be respected by others. They see injustice everywhere and keep tipping the scales of justice until they balance. As regards *what* is unjust or wrong, *they* will determine that themselves. When confronted by others they often refuse to listen. They preach their own idea of justice. They restructure situations and relationships to achieve their own goals and assume others do the same.

The holy idea of *compassion* can release EIGHTS from the trap of their own idea of justice. The compassion of Jesus reveals God's justice, i.e., the standards by which God governs the world. In teaching compassion to his followers Jesus gave Abba as model. We act as God acts toward enemies as well as toward friends. As Jesus said, "God makes his sun shine on the bad and good people alike and gives rain to those who do good and to those who do evil" (Mt 5:45). By abandoning themselves to God's ways of dealing with evil through compassion, EIGHTS are set free from their penchant to be judge over others and give up their over-confidence in knowing what is just. By saying, "Do not judge, and you will not be judged" (Mt 7:1), Jesus advises the suspension of judgment over others rather than imposing our notion of justice on them. For EIGHTS this is basic to abandoning themselves to God's reign over the world and letting God be ruler and judge. The revelation of God's compassion insists on a special attitude towards

enemies which expresses itself through mercy, forgiveness, non-violence and tolerance.

#9.

NINES are trapped by their idea of *self-
abasement.* They downgrade themselves and don't see
within themselves much that is of value. Lacking love
for themselves and unaware of their true importance
as persons, they think their energy has to come from
some outside source. They seek outside stimulation to
enliven them. Every aspect of an event is experienced
as having equal value, so NINES assign equal importance to the trivial and the significant.

The holy idea of *unconditional love* releases
NINES from the trap of their self-abasement. They
desperately need to feel deeply within themselves the
gospel message that they are unconditionally loved by
God and gifted with the Spirit. This needs to be more
than a belief; it needs to be a principle of action. To be
effective in moving them from indolence caused by
self-abasement, the idea of unconditional love needs
to be translated so they see themselves as truly lovable
because they are who they are. Only then do they love
in an outgoing, active way. For them above all, it is
true that *unless they know they are lovable they cannot
give love.* The idea of God's unconditional love calls
them to see their lovability. Once they find life within
themselves by being loved unconditionally, they reach
for real union with others rather than withdrawal from
life and its activities. For them abandonment to God
involves discovering the reality of unconditional love
as directed to them.

Affective Conversion: Passion Healed by Virtue

As a result of the intellectual conversion expressed by holy abandonment through the holy idea specific to each personality type, there follows what is called *affective conversion*, where the distortion of the passion is healed or rectified by virtue. FIGURE 17 presents the Enneagram of the passions, which was explained at length in Chapter 4 as an aspect of the "unbalanced self." FIGURE 18 presents the Enneagram of the virtues as pertaining to affective conversion.

Affective conversion follows from intellectual conversion because the heart center responds with passionate love to the good of fulfillment as seen by the head center. By placing self-fulfillment under God's domain or in God's hands by holy abandonment, the self is freed of the distortion in passionate love caused by the attitude of self-salvation. Now self-fulfillment is seen as a matter of being redeemed by God through a participation in the Kingdom of God. The distortion specific to each personality type is called a passion. The virtue healing or rectifying the passionate love of each type has a dominant disposition or attitude of the heart center.

Affective conversion in each personality type entails moving from the specific passion to the specific virtue. This movement or conversion occurs when the passion is abandoned in favor of the virtue which is a typical manifestation of essential love who is God. The following commentary on the affective conversion of each personality type will follow the numbers around the Enneagram from 1 to 9.

#1. Through holy abandonment ONES move

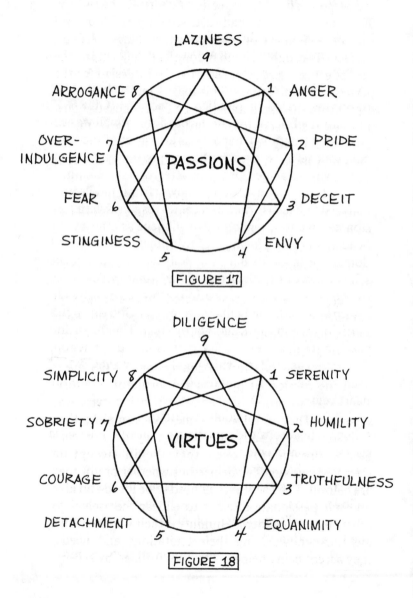

FIGURE 17

FIGURE 18

from the passion of anger to the virtue of *serenity*. Their passionate love had focussed on perfection, and they became angry or resentful when things were not perfect. Through holy abandonment they accept the idea of *growth* through process as God's design for the perfection of creatures. This makes imperfection acceptable to the passionate love of ONES because now it is seen as characteristic of any process of growth. Instead of looking for what is wrong in anything the heart now looks at what is already developed as good, slight as it may be, for sometimes good is present in seed form and hidden. In this way calmness or serenity comes to the heart center because greater growth can always happen in the future and conversion is always possible in anybody's heart. As they contemplate in their head center all the good they experience, ONES may become aware of a wonderful harmony of complementarity in creation as a sacred dance of opposites attracted to one another and then see themselves within that whole as drawn by the magnetism of an all-pervading Love.

#2. Through affective conversion TWOS move from the passion of pride to the virtue of *humility*. They were so proud of themselves; their service was superior. They developed a messiah complex; they could save everybody. Realizing they do not earn God's prevenient love, they begin accepting themselves as worthwhile persons whether or not they are helpful. They accept their need to be loved and give up their passionate attempt to endear themselves to others by serving them. Humility is their way to fulfillment. Acknowledging their limitations and needs, they accept being helped. They are fulfilled by accept-

ing the gift of a love they do not earn or control. Any other love does not fill their hearts. God's love and all true love is unconditional.

#3. For THREES affective conversion involves movement from the passion of deceit to the virtue of *truthfulness.* As long as they sought their fulfillment through achievements in competition with others their passionate love led them to justify even underhanded means for their own advancement. Holy abandonment results in THREES dedicating themselves to God's administration of the world. They now love truthfulness and openness because they see that the common good of society, to which they are dedicated, is best served by everyone "laying their cards out on the table," not by maneuvering to get some kind of advantage over another. Only by truthfulness do various individuals and groups in society come to trust one another and live in a spirit of interdependence by planning together in mutual helpfulness.

#4. Through holy abandonment, FOURS move from the passion of envy to the virtue of *equanimity.* Instead of seeking to draw attention to themselves through the specialness of their own refinement and being envious when another gets attention, they live their emotional lives in greater composure even under stress. Such equanimity results from their willingness to meet God in each event of daily life and from letting God draw from them their free response to the divine gifts at each now-moment. They see their fulfillment is being drawn into a mystery of life where God dwells rather than being recognized by another as having had unusually dramatic and tragic lives.

#5. Conversion to God in abandonment moves FIVES from the passion of stinginess to the virtue of *detachment.* They craved their solitude as time to study and reflect to satisfy their need to be filled with wisdom and not be ignorant or foolish. By accepting life as their teacher and getting involved in what is happening they have become detached from this clinging to their own privacy. It becomes less necessary for them to worry about storing up resources for future eventualities because they can live off the gifts of life day by day. They also become more able to share their inner world because they know it is the only way to enter the mystery of communion with others. This is a reality known only by participation.

#6. Through their holy abandonment SIXES move from the passion of fear to the virtue of *courage.* Finding their security in their divine adoption, they discover many of their previous fears seem to vanish. Changing structures, indefinite regulations and even illegal activities become less threatening to them because they see what God asks of them is never completely indicated by human institutions and precepts. They come to see that God wants them to promote values rather than to rely on tried and tested laws and norms.

Knowing that nothing can ever separate them from God's love (Rm 8:35-39), they discover in themselves courage to do new things on their own and to make decisions when matters are tentative and risky.

#7. Through holy abandonment SEVENS move from the passion of over-indulgence to the virtue of *sobriety.* They made a god of the pleasurable and

screened out negative realities to live in a fantasy world. By abandoning their lives to the hard work of co-creation they are able to sober up, to take on a life work which includes a practical implementation of Jesus' challenge to carry a daily cross. This leads SEVENS to the importance of being earnest through accepting the labor involved in giving birth to some of their dreams and ideals. In place of avoiding pain and seeking pleasures of the moment, they work even at the price of pain and frustration. They also come to accept the soberness of others who are engaged in the trials and labors of life.

#8. By abandonment to God EIGHTS move from the passion of arrogance to the virtue of *simplicity*. Once they place all judgment in God's hands and seek to imitate the attitude of Jesus toward injustice, they become able to take things at face value without probing and testing people. They become sensitive to the needs of others and more readily see that everyone has some value or gift. Jesus' words about becoming child-like to enter God's Kingdom (Mt 18:3) ring true for EIGHTS as the "natural child" within comes more to the fore. They increase their effectiveness in working for justice by identifying with God's own non-violent ways as exemplified by Jesus. They see the real wisdom and power of passive resistance to confront and unmask oppression.

#9. By conversion to the idea of holy love, NINES move from the passion of laziness to the virtue of *diligence*. The discovery of God's love for them awakens new energies within as they come to see their real worth as persons and discover yearning for self-development. Previously they were often tempted to

do nothing, thinking that whatever they did would not amount to much anyway. Once convinced of the great worth of their unique selves they take steps to learn skills and acquire credentials knowing that this is done by laboring hour by hour and day by day. In gratitude for God's love they seek to make some contribution to better the world because response to love shows itself in actions of service. It is astounding how NINES can be transformed from indolent spectators to patient, methodical workers. God's love *motivates* them.

Instinctual Conversion: Using Spiritual Discernment

When a person *reacts* to others and situations, those behaviors are expressions of habitual defenses rooted in what the Enneagram explains as the compulsion of each type. When a person is able to *respond* to others and situations their behaviors are manifestations of instinctual conversion at the gut center. There is an awakening to what St. Paul calls "the fruits of the Spirit," *viz.,* "love, joy, peace, patience, kindness, goodness, trustfulness, gentleness and self-control" (Gal 5:22f). As movements of consolation the fruits of the spirit also make the self more aware of contrary movements called desolation. The desire to notice and discern these movements arises from one's intellectual and affective conversion, for to live in God's hands means to move with the instinct given by God's indwelling Spirit. Spiritual discernment involves testing and tracking these movements of consolation and desolation to choose what to do and what not to do. To live on this instinctive level following the lead of the Spirit not only gives the self a sign of God's will but also results in a remarkable sense of well-being and inner joy.

These movements of consolation and desolation are characterized by *spontaneity* welling up from within. They arise from an innate sense of what is fitting or unfitting. Union with God through holy abandonment stamps the self with a basic orientation to God as Source of fulfillment and heals the distortion of passionate love. There is also a deep effect on the instincts of one's whole being; they are *given* by the indwelling Spirit a *connaturality* to the good, the right, the fulfilling. In his *Spiritual Exercises* St. Ignatius expresses this connaturality as follows:

> The good spirit, however, strengthens and encourages, consoles and inspires, establishes a peace and sometimes moves to a firm resolve. To lead a good life gives delight and joy, and no obstacle seems to be so formidable that it cannot be faced and overcome. The good spirit thereby continues an upright person's progress in the Lord.[29]

What St. Ignatius is saying is that it feels good to be good! On the other hand, to act contrary to what is in service to God feels bad—there is a desolation experienced. St. Ignatius puts this experience of desolation in the terminology of temptation:

> The evil spirit proposes to us all the problems and difficulties in living a good life. The evil spirit attempts to rouse a false sadness for things which will be missed, to bring about anxiety about persevering when we are so weak, to suggest innumerable roadblocks in walking the way of the Lord. And so the evil spirit tries discouragement and deception to deter us from growing in the Christ-life.[30]

According to the Ignatian discernment of spirits, there are three distinct experiences of consolation:[31]

(1) There is the experience of BEING ON FIRE.

Everything is seen in the context of God. No person or thing competes with the total gift of self to God in love. Others are simply loved in God, i.e., one loves God by loving them. This is a consuming consolation; there is no mistaking it because of its clarity and totality. It is a spine-tingling experience. This consolation seems exemplified in the sudden, all-consuming conversion of St. Paul (Ac 9:3-6).

(2) Another experience of consolation is that of BEING THANKFUL. This originates by comparing oneself with God, seeing oneself separate from God but very much loved. The experience of being thankful may be occasioned by a deep realization of being a sinner before God and yet being loved by God. *Tears* may accompany this consolation because one is saddened by infidelity to God, who is so good.

(3) A third experience of consolation is that of PEACE and STRENGTH. One senses a bold strengthening in faith, hope and love. There is joy in serving God and a deep peace just being in Abba's house. One *knows* that this present action is right and that it is okay to do it.

Corresponding to these distinct experiences of consolation are three contrary experiences of desolation:[32]

(1) There is the desolation of being enmeshed in TURMOIL of spirit, of being weighed down by heavy DARKNESS or WEIGHT. This is a forceful experience, for turmoil is a vortex spinning the helpless self round and round.

(2) Another experience of desolation is that of RESTLESSNESS and DISTASTE. One is unable to sit still, has a distaste for prayer or any spiritual activi-

ty and seems to lack faith, hope and love.

(3) A third experience of desolation is that of REBELLIOUSNESS, DESPAIR, and SELFISH-NESS. This is a very self-centered experience. One does not care about responding to God and even says, "I won't do it."

These three pairs of consolation and desolation may be seen as corresponding to the experiences typical of the three centers of the Enneagram:

(1) BEING ON FIRE and the TURMOIL of not getting anywhere are typical of the GUT CENTER.

(2) BEING THANKFUL is a heart-felt thing and DISTASTE and RESTLESSNESS characterize the back-and-forth movement typical of an emotional experience in the HEART CENTER.

(3) Abiding PEACE is a way of thinking: even though everything is going haywire, one senses it is still okay. Similarly the experience of DESPAIR and SELFISHNESS is also in the HEAD CENTER. One can feel the love of another but the head still can say, "I don't care." To be in REBELLIOUSNESS one has to think it out.

This superimposition of the three distinct experiences of consolation and desolation upon the three functioning centers of the Enneagram is shown in FIGURE 19 for the consolations and in FIGURE 20 for the desolations.

One may think that the consolation and desolation of each type corresponds to the *preferred center* of that type. Such is not the case, however, because conversion does not permit one to remain simply within one's center, and conversion flows from discernment. Conversion involves the self coming

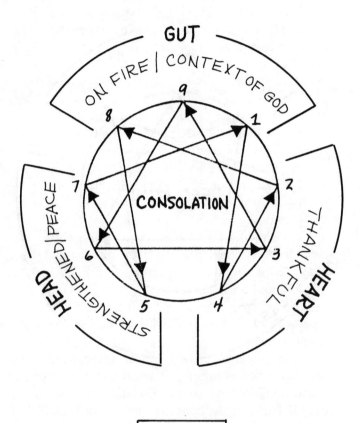

FIGURE 19

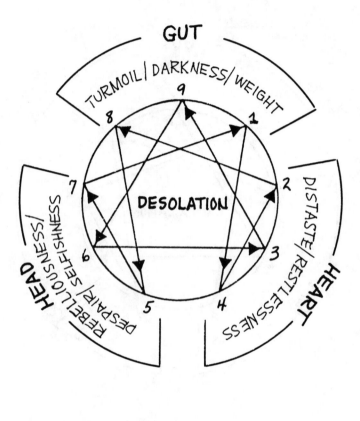

FIGURE 20

back into balance which happens by moving *against* the arrow of compulsion. It is from moving *against* the arrow that there arises the sense of fittingness that consolation represents. The consolation experience is that of the center entered by moving *against* the arrow. Similarly, moving *with* the arrow into greater compulsion brings desolation, and that experience of desolation belongs to the center entered by moving *with* the arrow. While reading the following commentary on the typical consolation of each personality type, refer to the arrows and centers shown in FIGURE 19 and FIGURE 20.

#1.

The consolation of ONES is the experience of PEACE, a characteristic of their HEAD CENTER, because moving toward the SEVEN *against* the arrow they move into the HEAD CENTER. For example, they continue to work hard but relax in it. They see they are on the road to perfection by working each day and they are at PEACE in thinking that it is okay if they don't achieve 100% perfection today.

The desolation of ONES is in the HEART CENTER because moving *with* the arrow they move toward the FOUR. The experience is that of DISTASTE and RESTLESSNESS. They become discouraged in trying to be perfect, stop trying and become moody. They have a feeling it is not *worth* the trouble to keep trying and say, "I've had it! But I should try one more time."

#2.

The consolation of TWOS is in the HEART CENTER because positive growth is moving *against* the arrow toward the FOUR. Their consolation is BE-ING THANKFUL. They know *they don't have to prove themselves,* even to God, who meets the needs they can't address in others. This frees them to attend to their own needs. They become more aware of those needs and decide to be wholesomely self-caring.

The desolation of TWOS is in the GUT CENTER. When they move *with* the arrow, they move toward the EIGHT. TWOS, who in consolation serve an enjoyable feast to friend and foe alike, ex-perience desolation as a profound DARKNESS in which they are unable to respond to any need. Even God has not appreciated their efforts.

#3.

The consolation of THREES is in the HEAD CENTER because they grow less bound by their mov-ing toward the SIX. They are consoled by being at PEACE. They acquire healthy self-doubt and say, "I don't have to do everything and not everything has to get done anyway."

The desolation of THREES is in the GUT CENTER because they move with the arrow of com-pulsion toward the NINE. Their desolation is to feel sucked down the drain in TURMOIL. They have a drive to keep moving but they are not going anywhere. They just keep moving in circles, spinning their wheels, doing non-essentials.

#4.

The consolation of FOURS is in the GUT CENTER because they move *against* the arrow by moving toward the ONE. Their consolation is an unbidden experience of BEING ON FIRE. They become less moody and more willing to take charge and do something. A unique *conviction* motivates the FOUR to significant action.

The desolation of FOURS is in the HEART CENTER because moving *with* the arrow is moving towards the TWO. Fours are natural contemplatives and experience desolation as a surprising DISTASTE for prayer. Their usual independence dissolves into a morass of self-pity.

#5.

The consolation of FIVES is in the GUT CENTER because they move toward the EIGHT by moving *against* the arrow. As they challenge reality and get involved in action, they are spurred on by conviction, boldness and BEING ON FIRE.

The desolation of FIVES is in the HEAD CENTER because their negative movement is *with* the arrow toward the SEVEN. The experience is that of SELFISHNESS. They flee from reality and retreat farther into their heads. They decide to be totally selfish and cling to their own theories.

#6.

The consolation of SIXES is in the GUT CENTER because they grow positively by moving *against* the arrow toward the NINE. Their consolation is to see things in the CONTEXT OF GOD, who loves everything and everyone. They become ON FIRE with self-assurance and are more spontaneous and zealous.

The desolation of SIXES is in the HEART CENTER because they move toward the THREE by moving *with* the arrow. The experience is that of RESTLESSNESS, which expresses itself in frenetic activity. They vacillate even within a well-defined task. For example, prayer becomes frantic ''Bible-thumbing.''

#7.

The consolation of SEVENS is in the HEAD CENTER because they move toward the FIVE by moving *against* the arrow. They are STRENGTHEN-ED: their ill-defined theology is revealed as substantive. The reality in the relationship they fantasized with God is affirmed.

The desolation of SEVENS is in the GUT CENTER because they move toward the ONE by moving *with* the arrow. The desolation experience is that of DARKNESS. They may want to feel consolation and don't, so they try to create it by their fantasy. They are able to fantasize feelings and thereby fool themselves and a spiritual director when describing their prayer experience. SEVENS can put on a good front and create the illusion of talking themselves out of hell. Once they finally face up to their inner desolation they may become like a kite plummeting down and crashing. Desolation oozes to consciousness as bitter resentment toward those closest to them.

#8.

The consolation of EIGHTS is in the HEART CENTER because they move *against* the arrow by moving toward the TWO. Their consolation is typically that of BEING THANKFUL. They do not like to face the fact that in spite of their outward behavior of strength they are marshmallows inside. A persistent God lavishes them with unmistakable whisperings of affection. Strengthened by God's gratuitous love, they continue in their unpopular prophetic vocation, THANKFUL to be chosen.

The desolation of EIGHTS is in the HEAD CENTER because they move *with* the arrow by moving toward the FIVE. The experience is that of SELFISHNESS. They give up being strong, collapse in a heap and disappear to sulk.

#9.

The consolation of NINES is in the HEART CENTER because their positive growth is in moving toward the THREE. The experience is that of BEING THANKFUL. They experience God loving them just as they are, even though they are not achievers. The response to God's unconditional love is heartfelt gratitude. They accept themselves as lovable and capable of loving.

The desolation of NINES is in the HEAD CENTER because they move *with* the arrow by moving toward the SIX. The experience is that of DESPAIR. Self-doubt smothers their concept of being worthwhile.

Totems and Colors as Symbols of the Redeemed Types

FIGURE 21 portrays the Enneagram of the redeemed types symbolized by totems and FIGURE 22 as symbolized by colors. This way of concluding the material on conversion of the personality types provides some amusement but also some added insight, especially that of the particular *beauty* and strength of each type.

#1.

Redeemed ONES are characterized by the ANT. Ants are extremely industrious and well organized to achieve a purpose. Each has its specific job to do. They are able to lift immense loads many times their weight. They communicate only at close range by touching antennae. Like ants, redeemed ONES are well organized: they know what needs to be done and readily cooperate with others to bring things into being. They communicate at close range by inviting people to the ideal rather than by shoving or pressuring.

The symbolic color of ONES is SILVER. Their personalities are like brilliant reflected light; they have a *clear, sharp presence.*

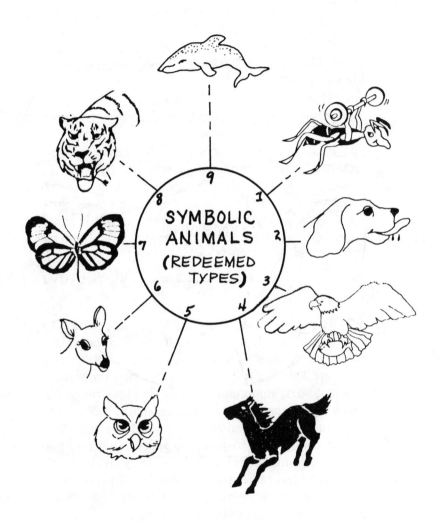

FIGURE 21

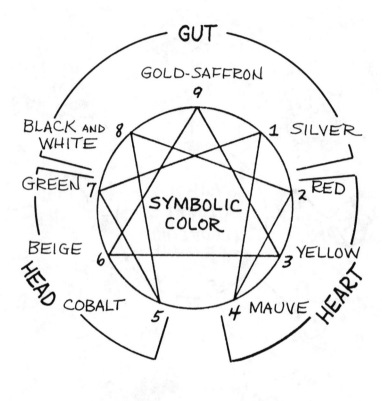

FIGURE 22

#2.

Redeemed TWOS are characterized by the IRISH SETTER. Setters are warm in color and the gloss on their coat attracts notice. They exude a real warmth and remember people they like. They are extremely loyal and rarely greet anyone with animosity. They are "emotionally" effusive, overjoyed to see another and they can lick a person to death. They are always ready to follow a friend.

The TWOS' symbolic color is RED. Red is the heart color, the color of warmth, feeling and intensity. On the other hand, there are many places where red cannot be seen; darkness causes it to appear blue and remain quite unnoticeable. In the same way redeemed TWOS are able to pull back from their intensity. Through their healing and conversion they are able to give the warmth of love without strings attached. They respect the freedom of the other. They are open to whatever love another may choose to give them and to respond to it warmly and with gratitude as a gift to them.

#3.

Redeemed THREES are characterized by the BALD EAGLE. Eagles are larger than life; with a wingspan of six feet their size is simply overwhelming. They are beautiful in appearance; for even though their plummage is not striking, its variations of browns are attractive. Their white head and white tail feathers make their identity unmistakable. They have an economy of motion, rarely flapping their wings.

They maintain life-long relationships, mating for life and building annually on their original nest. They wear the mask of a predator but are often scavengers eating dead fish. Like eagles, redeemed THREES are at ease with who they are. Through conversion they focus on God and the divine administration of the world rather than on manipulation of others. They have developed real loyalty to their friends.

The symbolic color of THREES is BRIGHT YELLOW, the yellow of a school bus. It is a color that cannot be ignored; it can be seen under all conditions, even fog or in the dark. It is not a pretty color but is certainly very functional. Like the bright yellow, THREES stand out as persons especially when healed and redeemed of their compulsion.

#4.

Redeemed FOURS are characterized by the BLACK STALLION or BLACK BEAUTY. Such horses are sleek, dark and walk tall. Free spirits, they toss their manes in the wind. They may decide to gallop anytime; they frisk, bolt and then stop. They have a variety of gaits, each with a special name. They gaze at people and come to meet them with a self-possessed grace. They take sugar but prefer apples which have a special kind of sugar. Like black horses, redeemed FOURS remain special, with a self-possessed grace.

They know they are the unique creation of a loving God. They have come to understand that how they feel does fit the situation at hand and they know what is good when they see it.

The symbolic color of FOURS is MAUVE. This color is in the purple range but cannot be identified exactly. Being subtle and understated, it connotes the special. FOURS typically dress understatedly but always with exquisite taste and often in a solid dark color.

#5.

Redeemed FIVES are characterized by the OWL. Owls have two positions: the first is an alert rest while watching with big eyes; the second is their silent, deadly swoop to make a kill. They do not move until they have their prey in sight and then they come down right on target. Their eyes and ears are adapted to receive information even when in flight. Everything, even their flight feathers, is adapted for silent motion. They have an amazing ability to tackle huge animals. They eat only what is needed and regurgitate unusable parts. Redeemed FIVES no longer go sneaking about like foxes trying to understand everything without getting involved. Like owls they can be at rest while remaining alert. By holy abandonment they are aware they do not have to understand everything and that divine providence has prepared them for involvement.

The symbolic color of FIVES is COBALT, which is a deep, intense blue. Cobalt used to be called the "demon of the mines"; it was deep down in the earth and because people didn't understand its value, they found it too troublesome to mine.

#6.

Redeemed SIXES are characterized by the DEER. Deer are always on the alert. Their ears can be turned to funnel sound. They have large sensitive noses which pick up a variety of aromas. They have the ability to flex their skin and shake off biting flies. Their legs are like coiled springs, ready for any danger, and they need take only a few graceful leaps to reach safety. There they stop and inspect their intruder. Deer are uniquely adapted to survive. In winter if no other forage is available, they are able to eat bark. A starving doe re-absorbs one of her two fetuses to insure a live birth. Deer face predators as a herd and rarely is one seen alone. Like deer, redeemed SIXES are always ready and alert to avoid danger. They have great ability to survive amid the difficulties of life because they draw strength from their group. They have learned to live in a relaxed way by discovering that God is loyal and faithful and that their salvation does not depend simply on themselves.

The symbolic color of SIXES is BEIGE. Like beige, SIXES are adaptable anywhere. Although not offensive, they don't blend into the woodwork either.

#7.

Redeemed SEVENS are characterized by the BUTTERFLY. Though beautiful, butterflies are actually monochromatic. Their colors are reflections of the sun's light on the facets of their wings. They are very subtle and touch down lightly. They have specialized tongues and are needed by flowers to further life through the distribution of pollen. They are born as the result of a long period of dullness and come to life only after a great struggle to emerge. Like butterflies, redeemed SEVENS come to recognize that the beauty they radiate is not their own but a reflection of God's presence refracted by the joys and sorrows of life. They know that God sees and cares even when things are painful, and they can find reason to hope.

The symbolic color of SEVENS is GREEN which is a color of vitality and life.

#8.

Redeemed EIGHTS are characterized by the TIGER. There are very few tigers in the world. They are very large animals but despite their size and power they are camouflaged. They stalk carefully, waiting for the right moment before they pounce. They are able to bring down large prey and are selective in what they eat. They like to swim and are at home in a variety of environments, whether in the snow or in the tropics. They are loyal to their mates and play fondly with their cubs. Redeemed EIGHTS are like tigers; they are beautiful and strong. When converted, their power as persons is more camouflaged. They are loyal to family and friends and sensitive to people. They are able to be playful in a childlike way. Having accepted the reign of God's justice, EIGHTS accept being who they are created to be. They are able to be at home in any place. They do have power but they can wait for the right moment to use it.

EIGHTS have two symbolic colors, both BLACK and WHITE. These are the extremes of color.

EIGHTS are either-or persons.

#9.

Redeemed NINES are characterized by the POR-POISE. Porpoises are a vulnerable contradiction, being air-breathing "fish." They swim with a regular motion and momentum. They look intelligent and are eager to learn. They willingly cooperate with others. They maintain constant communication with one another. Known to be peacemakers of the sea, they prod sharks away from human swimmers. Like porpoises, redeemed NINES have the ability to relax and move with things as they are because they have discovered their own worth. They like to be part of a group through which they participate in life. Wherever they are they are peacemakers.

The symbolic color of NINES is GOLD or SAF-FRON. Saffron is the gold-yellow color worn by Buddhist monks. It is a peaceful and restful color. Gold is a very precious metal. It is found deep within the earth and is difficult to extract. NINES might be surprised to be compared with gold because they have thought so little of themselves. Having discovered through God's love that they are very gifted and lovable, they can see themselves as a precious gift of God to the world.

EPILOGUE

The story is told of a Zulu girl who lived in a village where all the marriageable young women wore necklaces. Hers, however, was different and more beautiful than that worn by any of the others. As a result the other girls became jealous of her. One day, as she was walking alone along the river, she met a group of the other girls, who told her they had all thrown their necklaces into the river as an offering to the river god. They urged her to make the same sacrifice. So the girl took off her beautiful necklace and cast it into the river. Then all the girls laughed as they pulled out their necklaces from their pockets and ran off gleefully. In great sadness the girl continued to walk slowly along the river; but then she heard a voice within her say, "Jump in!" So she jumped into the river at that very spot. At the bottom of the river she swam into a cave where she met an old woman who had been much hurt by life. The woman said to her, "Kiss my scars and sores." The girl said, "I will do so gladly." When the girl had done so, suddenly the woman was completely healed and she looked young and beautiful again. The woman said to the girl, "Since you have done this for me, I will make you invisible to the demons so that they cannot harm you." At that very moment the girl heard the voice of a demon saying, "I smell flesh; I smell flesh." The demon, however, could not see her and went away. Then the woman gave her a new necklace, even more beautiful than the one she had lost.

The girl went back to the village. When the other girls saw her, they were very surprised and asked her where she had obtained the beautiful necklace. She said that after they had left her, she had walked alone along the river until she heard a voice within her say, "Jump in!" She said she jumped into the river at that very spot and entered a cave where she met an old woman who gave her the necklace. The other girls asked where that exact spot was that she had jumped into the river and she told them. So all the girls ran down to the river and jumped into the river just at that place. They entered a cave and met an old woman who had been much hurt by life. She asked the girls to kiss her sores and scars that they might be healed. The girls, however, were filled with repulsion at the sight of the lady and refused to do as she said. Just at that moment they heard the voice of a demon saying, "I smell flesh; I smell flesh." Since they could readily be seen by the demon, he at once devoured them all.

To undertake the study of the Enneagram for one's own enlightenment is to risk becoming like the Zulu girl who threw her cherished necklace into the river. There is a casting aside of something up to now deemed very important to one's pride and dignity. A journey alone into the self begins, which leads to memories of past hurts, especially from the vulnerable years of one's childhood. It was then that one's personality type was formed as a reaction to disappointments and felt neglect from others. These hurts are still there. They need to be befriended along with their consequences in later life. One has the power to heal past hurts by going back to them in memory with forgiveness and compassion, to kiss them as it were. Such a "disarmament of the heart" can remove the hurts so that the self can come forth with a new sense of pride and confidence based on self-enlightenment freeing one from the dark side of the self. As a consequence, one is no longer in danger of being devoured by that dark side. The compulsion's presence is still felt, but now one knows always how to escape its clutches.

NOTES

1. Sam Keen, "A conversation about ego destruction with Oscar Ichazo," *Psychology Today,* Vol. VII, No. 2, July 1973, p. 64.

2. J.G. Bennett, *The Enneagram*, Coombe Springs Press, England, 1974. Introduction explains mathematical properties combined in the Enneagram symbol; i.e., the significance of zero and the summation of the recurring decimals resulting from the division of one by three and seven.

3. St. Paul often presents *sin* as a power which enslaves a person. Cf Rm 7:14-23.

4. Sam Keen, *op cit,* p. 67.

5. In Christian thought, being freed from sin can only occur by the acknowledgement of being a sinner. Liberation from the sin already begins once one has recognized the need for forgiveness and healing. Cf 1 Jn 1:8-10.

6. These statements are adapted from the unpublished doctoral dissertation of Jerome P. Wagner, "A descriptive, reliability, and validity study of the Enneagram personality typology" (Doctoral dissertations, Loyola University of Chicago, 1981). *Dissertations Abstracts International,* 1981, 41, 4664A.

7. *Ibid.*

8. *Ibid.*

9. *Ibid.*

10. *Ibid.*

11. *Ibid.*

12. *Ibid.*

13. *Ibid.*

14. *Ibid.*

15. *Ibid.*

16. *Orthodox Faith,* bk 2, lect 1. Early Christian writers generally held that the essence of our salvation is from the divine Logos being united with our humanity; hence, if any part of humanness were not assumed by the Logos, it could not be saved, i.e., united with God. This was often said to those denying full humanness in Jesus. The writers insisted on Jesus having not only a human body but also human thoughts and feelings, such as anger, pleasure, fear, sadness, and affection.

17. Cf Mt 21:12f; Mk 11:15-17; Lk 19:45f.

18. Cf Jn 8:28; Mt 27:54; Ac 2:36-38.

19. Sam Keen, *op cit,* p. 67.

20. Tad Dunne's material in this book is derived from his lectures in his course on Prayer at Creighton University, Omaha, Nebraska, in the summer session of 1980. Tables I and II are directly from his course.

21. *Ibid.*

22. *Ibid.*

23. Sam Keen, *op cit,* p. 67.

24. This figure adapted from John C. Lilly and Joseph E. Hart, "The Arica Training," in C. Tart (Ed.), *Transpersonal Psychologies.* Harper and Row, New York, 1975, p. 333.

25. Pyotr D. Ouspensky, *In Search of the Miraculous,* Hartcourt, Brace & World, New York, 1949, p. 114.

26. In the document on "The Church in the Modern World of Vatican II," this was expressed in terms of God creating human persons as ends in themselves (GS, 24).

27. The notion of "the sacrament of the present moment" was presented by Jean-Pierre de Caussade, S.J., in his posthumous book, *Abandonment to Divine Providence,* Image Books, New York, 1975.

28. Gabriel Marcel is noted for his definition of mystery as that which can be known only by participation in its reality. Cf Sam Keen, *Gabriel Marcel,* John Knox Press, Richmond, Virginia, 1967, pp. 20-22.

29. David L. Fleming, S.J., *The Spiritual Exercises of St. Ignatius: A Literal Translation and A Contemporary Reading,* Institute of Jesuit Sources, St. Louis, 1978. "Guidelines for the Discernment of Spirits," [315].

30. *Ibid.*

31. *Ibid,* [316].

32. *Ibid,* [317].